TRANSFORMING SEXUAL NARRATIVES

Transforming Sexual Narratives offers readers the opportunity to address complex sexual problems through Narrative Relational Sex Therapy (NRST), an original approach that Suzanne Iasenza has developed during twenty-five years of clinical practice.

This method presents a deeper, richer way of thinking about sexual challenges that has enabled clients to successfully rewrite their mistaken narratives to reclaim pleasure, intimacy, and satisfaction in their erotic lives. Drawing on the strengths of three very different therapeutic traditions – psychoanalytic, couple and family systems, and sex therapy – it delivers a fresh and dynamic way of understanding the complex interrelationship among personal, social, cultural, and familial sexual narratives. Chapters include conversations with diverse couples and individuals from all kinds of backgrounds and cultures, who exist in every kind of body, and in each case show how unconscious and harmful narratives can be transformed into healthy and pleasurable sex lives.

This essential guide will help therapists to identify their client's secret sexual stories and enable them to rewrite their inner narratives and relationship with sexuality for the better. Sex therapists will be able to integrate a relational perspective into behavioral treatment, individual and couple therapists will be able to weave sexuality into general psychotherapy, and psychoanalysts will be able to use the sexual history to identify early dynamics that affect adult intimacy.

Suzanne Iasenza is a psychologist and sex therapist based in New York City. She is a faculty member at the Institute for Contemporary Psychotherapy and Psychoanalysis, the Ackerman Institute for the Family, and the Adelphi University Post-Graduate Program in Psychoanalysis.

TRANSFORMING SEXUAL NARRATIVES

A Relational Approach to Sex Therapy

Suzanne Iasenza

Routledge
Taylor & Francis Group

NEW YORK AND LONDON

First published 2020
by Routledge
52 Vanderbilt Avenue, New York, NY 10017

and by Routledge
2 Park Square, Milton Park, Abingdon, Oxon, OX14 4RN

Routledge is an imprint of the Taylor & Francis Group, an informa business

© 2020 Taylor & Francis

Library of Congress Cataloging-in-Publication Data
A catalog record for this title has been requested

ISBN: 978-0-367-20574-4 (hbk)
ISBN: 978-0-367-20575-1 (pbk)
ISBN: 978-0-429-26237-1 (ebk)

Typeset in Perpetua
by Apex CoVantage, LLC

For
Barbara,
Edwin & Fredy
Transformers Extraordinaire

CONTENTS

CONTENTS

ACKNOWLEDGMENTS

Writing a book is a community process. Many inspiring thinkers, writers, and clinicians inform this book, serving as my compasses and lighthouses while navigating the ever-shifting waters of sexuality. One worth mentioning here whose words lead the way is poet Audre Lorde, who by example and through her work reminds us that we are all more than our differences and that true liberation resides in breaking our silences.

I am foremost grateful to my clients over the years who demonstrated the courage to break their silences with me, often through leaps of faith, in the service of greater personal and relational transformation and connection. They have been my most profound teachers.

My students, supervisees, and colleagues have challenged me to translate and explain, to demonstrate and adjust the ideas and techniques contained in this book. I am grateful for all the feedback over the years — always offered with good humor and support.

In particular I am indebted to the members of my feminist sexuality study group: Deborah Berry, Isabel Kaplan, Meg Kaplan, Brunhild Kring, and Susan Mahler, who provide the most nourishing holding environment a therapist could ask for within which to share the pains and pleasures of the work, while also creating opportunities to laugh and play in the world. And to Leonore Tiefer, who started it all many years ago.

I give thanks to the members of the Institute for Contemporary Psychotherapy, my institutional home, who over the past twenty-plus years embraced and supported the development of my Summer Sexuality Series course. In particular, I am grateful to Joanne Spina, Bob Najaar, Eddie Pabon, Sheila Josephson, Ron Taffel, Ian Kerner, and Tobin Berlinger.

My past and present colleagues in the Ackerman Institute's Project on Couples and Intimacies led by my friend and colleague, Michele Scheinkman, have been a superb Greek Chorus of diverse stimulating voices who have enriched, expanded, and supported my work: Tom Cronin, Susan Lemor, Keren Ludwig, Peggy Papp, Jean Malpas, and Dorimar Morales.

My deep thanks to my agent, Kevin O'Connor, who supported this book from the beginning. And to my editor, Clare Ashworth, and her staff at Routledge who helped me through the process.

To Rich Simon, Marian Sandmaier, and the editors at *Psychotherapy Networker* who encouraged me to develop parts of my work on sexual narratives in its early stages. Thanks to Evan Imber Black, as editor at *Family Process*, who invited me to write about the complexity of sexuality.

Thanks to Laura Markowitz, Cindy Barrilleaux, and Al Desetta, who patiently gave writing advice and helped me put words together on the page that made sense, and Meg Kaplan, who generously read through and commented on the entire draft. Jane Ryder helped with literary advice and technical support just when I needed it.

And finally, my family and friends suffered through hearing endless updates about "the book," and tolerated long periods of silence and my absence at social gatherings. My parents, Nick and Rosie, provided support from the beginning that launched and still sustains my work. My sister Annie offers unconditional love and interest. Edwin and Fredy's love always restores me, and Barbara makes it all possible and worthwhile.

CREDITS

I am grateful to the following publishers for granting permission to reprint excerpts of my previous writing for this book:

In the Family magazine:
Suzanne Iasenza (April 1998), "Who Decides What is Healthy Sexuality?"

Rowman & Littlefield:
Suzanne Iasenza (2006), "Low Sexual Desire in Gay, Lesbian, and Heterosexual Peer Marriages." In J.S. Scharff & D.E. Scharff (Eds.), *New Paradigms for Treating Relationships*.

John Wiley & Sons:
Suzanne Iasenza (2010), *What is Queer About Sex: Expanding Sexual Frames in Theory and Practice*.

Psychotherapy Networker:
Suzanne Iasenza (January/February 2016), "Transforming Sexual Narratives: From Dysfunction to Discovery."

"This is simply a wonderfully written book that acknowledges the unruly multidimensionality of sex and offers a rich, deep understanding of sexual issues and the stories that shape our sex lives; a clear way forward to eroticism that is about pleasure, not just performance; and intimate connection rather than recipes for endless novelty. Note this as essential reading for every sex therapist and couple counsellor!"

— **Sue Johnson**, author of *Hold Me Tight: Seven Conversations for a Lifetime of Love*, Canada

"Suzanne Iasenza has written a unique and challenging book which should be on every clinician's shelf, especially those working with non-traditional individuals and couples. Her relational approach to sex therapy, focused on transforming sexual narratives, is a comprehensive approach combining psychodynamic, couple, and queer perspectives. The emphasis on willingness as the key to desire, creating a sexual menu, mindfulness narrative touch, kink, and sexual resilience provides an empathic, respectful perspective on individual and couple sex therapy. Particularly important is confronting simplistic understandings and the pathologizing of sexual variations. Dr. Iasenza confronts secrecy and shame as she encourages clients to make meaning of the complex themes from childhood and create a meaningful narrative about themselves, and their relational and sexual lives. Sexuality enhances mastery and satisfaction."

— **Barry McCarthy**, Professor of Psychology, American University, USA

"On the topic of sex therapy, there is no one I trust more than Dr. Suzanne Iasenza. She is at home with patients who are lesbian, gay, queer, straight, non-binary, cisgender, and trans. Wherever someone lands in what we might call the sexual diaspora, Iasenza is able to meet them with a capacious clinical wisdom. Relying on notions from narrative therapy, family systems, and psychoanalysis, she offers case examples that help couples and therapists move past outdated, normative goals to a model focused on willingness and pleasure. This is no less than a step towards the cultural redefinition of Eros."

— **Deborah Anna Luepnitz**, PhD, psychoanalyst and author of *Schopenhauer's Porcupines*, USA

"Never before has the realm of the practice of sex therapy been explored in such depth, breadth, and sensitivity. Suzanne Iasenza demonstrates the wide range of therapeutic interventions that can be called up in the process of healing and integration. She provides the reader with a lucid conceptual base and a detailed account of practical ways of doing sex therapy using her innovative model. She helps us rethink what is healthy sex, doing so with exquisite sensitivity to the cultural and socio-political issues that impact us all. This is essential reading for every couple therapist."

— **Lois Braverman**, MSW, President Emeritus,
Ackerman Institute for the Family, USA

"With *Transforming Sexual Narratives*, Suzanne Iasenza has written an instant classic – a book that should be read by every clinician, not just those who consider themselves sex therapists. Weaving together the most current psychoanalytic theories, family systems theory, and a genuine understanding of the intersubjective nature of human experience, she builds a compelling narrative that builds to her own, very unique Relational Theory of Sex Therapy. Finally, we have an answer to that often-asked question "what is it that sex therapists actually do?" Iasenza not only tells us, but tells us how to do it effectively. The book is devoid of jargon, written with empathy and a directness accessible to all, and filled with meaningful clinical examples that bring her concepts alive. Debunking prevalent sexual myths like sex with strangers always lacks intimacy, Iasenza critiques the ubiquitous Desire-Arousal-Orgasm Model of sexual experience, that imposes a rigid linear scheme on what's actually a complex multidimensional process. Most clients, she asserts, unknowingly internalize this model as the only model of "healthy" sexuality. The party line, she suggests, kills the party, and she offers a new model that includes each individual's lived experience. I cannot recommend *Transforming Sexual Narratives* more highly. It will change how we all work."

— **Sandra Kiersky**, PhD, co-editor, *Sexualities Lost and Found*,
International Universities Press, Institute for the
Psychoanalytic Study of Subjectivity, USA

"Suzanne Iasenza is a master clinician, an inspiring teacher, and an excellent writer. In *Transforming Sexual Narratives*, she builds upon earlier theoretical and clinical approaches to develop a comprehensive, practical, and effective methodology for achieving transformation. Iasenza offers a framework for Narrative Relational Therapy and a guide to practice with practical examples to share her professional experience with individuals and couples. She shows how to do work that gets to the root of the problem and enables therapists and clients to examine the long-hidden core aspects of individual experience and the sexual persona. Her approach embraces the full complexity of a person and recognizes the depth of sexuality developed over a lifetime. She demonstrates how to clear obstacles and break patterns. This book provides therapists and patients with a clear vision that the change they seek is perfectly possible by stressing the difference between desire and willingness, between history and fate, between limiting beliefs and real possibilities. *Transforming Sexual Narratives* is a genuinely helpful book that will transform clinical practice with people of all genders and sexual orientations, solo and partnered. It challenges assumptions, increases clinical competence, elevates our approach to human sexuality, and can truly transform clinical practice. As a sex therapist who works with individuals and couples I am energized and eager to get to work with these transformational tools."

— **Katherine Rachlin**, PhD, clinical psychologist, AASECT Diplomate of Sex Therapy, USA

"Suzanne Iasenza's *Transforming Sexual Narratives* beautifully details an approach to sexual difficulty that has both far-reaching breadth and stunning depth. She creatively combines elements from a range of important contributors from behavioral therapy, psychodynamic approaches, sexology, and mindfulness, to name a few. She applies the resulting tools to today's broad variety of sexualities – to partnered and unpartnered sex, gay and straight sex, and polyamory and single sex in order to enable the clinician reader to develop an informed, flexible, and tensile capacity to face the many issues that are the staple of modern work with sexual difficulty. Iasenza's widely informed and integrated approach will enhance the work of clinicians of all stripes who dedicate themselves to working with sex and relationships."

— **David Scharff**, MD, co-founder and former director, the International Psychotherapy Institute; former president, The American Association of Sex Educators, Counselors and Therapists; and chair of the International Psychoanalytic Association's Committee on Couple and Family Psychoanalysis, USA

"Sex therapy has evolved since the pioneering work of William Masters and Virginia Johnson. Their research was heavily focused on the physiological process that occurred in the body during intercourse and at the point of orgasm. But as someone once said, sex is not what you have between your legs but what you have between your ears. How do our thoughts, the narratives we tell ourselves and others, promote or interfere with healthy sexual functioning? Given the state of sexuality education in the United States, it is not surprising that many people believe that they are the only ones who feel or think the way they do. In *Transforming Sexual Narratives: A Relational Approach to Sex Therapy*, Dr. Iasenza demonstrates through the use of case histories how a client's mistaken sexual narratives can be transformed 'to reclaim intimacy and satisfaction in their erotic lives.' Dr. Iasenza's approach to sex therapy offers a valuable guide for any psychotherapist who has clients with sexual problems."

— **Herb Samuels**, PhD, past president, Society for the Scientific Study of Sexuality, USA

"Suzanne Iasenza's new book, *Transforming Sexual Narratives: A Relational Approach to Sex Therapy*, builds upon her extraordinary body of previous clinically informed work on sexually conflicted, low desire, and otherwise struggling varieties of couples that are seeking an appropriate holding environment for sorting out and improving their intimate relationships. Her relational approach (NRST) embodies the best of scientific contributions from sexology, and sexual disorders literature and practice, but her contemporary psychoanalytic, clinical-technical wisdom captures the essential narratives of lived couple experience, past and present. What is truly transformative in these pages, for the beginning and experienced couple's therapist, is how her chapters weave the sexual and interpersonal histories of each partnership into a therapeutic potential, opening a space for new emotional experience that both informs and improves empathic understanding, for couple use, enriching their relational mosaic. While readers of this book can learn about skills when working with sexual difficulties of couples, the strength of her work is in its humble translation of the internal and external worlds of her treatment couples. Dr. Iasenza embraces and expects a psychological-emotional exposure to occur and utilizes transferences and countertransference to cull the necessary underbelly of neglected, traumatized, and repressive elements so interpretive and technical measures can be applied. This book adds a necessary component of relationally sound clinical material for use in working with troubled couples presenting disorders of desire, and other symptoms of disappointment and dissatisfying interpersonal relations. I recommend it without hesitation. In fact, I recommend reading it twice."

— **Carl Bagnini**, LCSW, BCD, senior and founding faculty, The International Psychotherapy Institute, and faculty, The Adelphi Derner Institute Post-graduate and Doctoral Programs in Psychoanalysis and Couple Therapy, USA; author of *Keeping Couples in Treatment: Working From Surface to Depth*

INTRODUCTION

I've been a sex therapist for over twenty-five years, working with individuals and couples of all sexualities and genders, from all kinds of backgrounds and cultures, and who exist in every kind of body. I've worked with heterosexual people, LGBTQ people, people with disabilities, and people whose sexualities are "kinky" and polyamorous. Yet despite these differences, the stories I hear from clients are often strikingly similar:

"We're the broken couple. Our best days of sex are behind us."
"I'm not desirable because I gained weight (or: my breasts are too small;"
"I can't stay hard; my skin is too dark)."
"I'm damaged goods in bed because of the childhood abuse I suffered."
"I'm a perv because I need to fantasize about something else when I'm in bed with my partner."

There are two kinds of sexual narratives: the ones we're aware of and are ashamed to admit, and the ones we keep secret even from ourselves. If sexual narratives were only occurring in the conscious mind, we might deal with the problematic ones in a rational way – try to "out-think" them, so to speak. But many sexual narratives – the ones that often do the most harm – are buried so deeply in our unconscious we're not even aware of them.

Transforming Sexual Narratives was written to guide psychotherapists in how to work with clients who believe they're the only ones with sexual problems, who view themselves as broken, wrong, "off," sick, or perverted. This book distills the wisdom I've gained from working with clients who have successfully transformed mistaken narratives to reclaim intimacy and satisfaction in their erotic lives. It can help sex therapists integrate a relational perspective into behavioral treatment. Individual and couple therapists may use this as a

1

guide for how to introduce and include sexuality into general psychotherapy. And psychoanalysts can use the sexual history to identify early dynamics that affect adult intimacy.

Countless books and articles promise the "fix" for sexual problems through better communication, the latest hormones, or new sexual positions. We live in the age of the Google search, with readily available pornography for all sexual tastes. The apps on our phones make it easy to date or hook up almost immediately. Yet the clients I've worked with for nearly three decades still feel isolated and imprisoned by their sexual narratives. Mere sexual freedom hasn't been the answer to the problems I encounter in my practice. Surveys consistently find that half or more of couples are not satisfied with their sex lives.

Over the years I've come to realize that neither therapists nor clients were shining enough light on sexual narratives, nor were therapists understanding the harm they caused by clinging to outmoded models of addressing sexual difficulties. The approach I've developed, which I call Narrative Relational Sex Therapy (NRST), presents a deeper way of thinking about sexual challenges and solutions, delivering a dynamic approach to helping people understand the complex interrelationship among their personal, social, cultural, and familial sexual narratives. The goal of this book is to make the methods and insights of NRST available to therapists and the programs that train them. Written in an accessible style, *Transforming Sexual Narratives* will help therapists guide their clients in rewriting their unconscious and harmful narratives by employing the NRST method. Using anonymized case histories from my practice, I provide detailed examples of how this rewriting can be done, what it looks like, what it sounds like, and how it takes place with couples or single people (which means NRST is also a relevant approach in individual therapy). I integrate ideas from many different theorists – psychoanalysts, couple and family therapists, and sexologists – to demonstrate how you can apply these methods.

I'll explain how clients can transform traditional linear sexual narratives that stand in the way of a healthy and pleasurable sex life. I'll expand definitions of sexual enjoyment and show therapists how they can help clients revise the "must-have-orgasm-for-sex-to-count" narrative. I'll demonstrate how you can help couples recognize and remove barriers that prevent them from connecting. Throughout the book I use non-binary, gender-neutral pronouns – "they," "them," "their" – except in case examples involving cisgender clients (those whose gender matches the sex they were assigned at birth).

Part 1 of the book (Chapters 1 to 5) describes the NRST therapeutic process, which involves identifying and transforming sexual narratives, the tools and techniques I use to do so, and anonymized case examples that tangibly illustrate how the process works.

Part 2 (Chapters 6 to 10) examines how the NRST method can be used by therapists to navigate complex and challenging sexual issues, such as polyamory, kink, emotional sadism in relationships, and solo sexuality. In case examples all identities are well-disguised to protect the confidentiality of clients.

The Hidden Power of Sexual Narratives

Secret sexual narratives have tremendous power in shaping ideas about and enjoyment of sexuality. For years Clara had been telling herself she was broken, abnormal, and a fraud because she couldn't have an orgasm during sex. She had faked them during a twenty-five-year marriage to a man that ended in divorce, and now she was faking them with her new lover, a woman she intended to marry. I found it poignant that this educated, smart, and successful person truly believed her revelation would shock me. I can't count the number of times I've heard variations on her story in my practice.

"I've read up on my condition," Clara said, looking miserable, "and I think I must be frigid or sexually immature."

I told her she was neither of those things. The idea that her problem might not be a problem left her momentarily speechless.

For Clara, "normal" sex had to culminate in orgasm. She didn't realize that having one isn't necessary for a satisfying sex life. It wasn't Clara who was "broken," but rather the stories she had been telling herself for years about sex. These kinds of problematic stories can be unpacked and worked through, using the tools of NRST. Doing so enables someone to experience sexual agency in the present – the ability to heal from false narratives and to enjoy sexuality.

Even the hardest cases can be transformed, including clients who face significant health challenges or have a history of abuse. *Transforming Sexual Narratives* draws much of its foundation from the work of Robert Stoller (1979, 1985) and other pioneers, including Alfred Kinsey (Kinsey, Pomeroy, & Martin, 1948; Kinsey, Pomeroy, Martin, & Gebhard, 1953), who normalized what was once considered "aberrant" sexual behavior. Stoller's seminal insight was that *all* sexuality – whether it's monogamous heterosexual sex in the missionary position, kinky sex, or polyamorous arrangements – is an attempt to master childhood conflicts and trauma. Illuminating how these conflicts and trauma are expressed and encountered within ourselves and with others holds the key to liberation from narratives that limit and bind us. Kinsey and his colleagues contributed the continuum to our understanding of sexual orientation that began a paradigm shift from binary to more fluid understandings of sexuality and gender. Family therapist Michael White (1989, 1995, 2007), an originator of Narrative Therapy, asserted that people carry many interwoven narratives about the self that present in therapy. If such narratives are treated as stories constructed by the contexts of people's lives rather than fixed (problematic) qualities about themselves or their relationships, people will be freer to re-author more fulfilling lives.

Where do troublesome narratives, these inner saboteurs, come from?

Sexual narratives are not generic. They are as unique and individual as one's DNA. They sprout from one's particular history, culture, relationships, and family, and then flourish in the fertile ground of one's hopes and fears, dreams and disappointments.

One's earliest narratives of sexuality develop well before learned language. Though rarely remembered, one's first experiences as an infant consist of physical sensation and pleasure. The skin tingles with touch; tiny ears soak up comforting murmurs and heartbeats; the tongue experiences the sweet delights of flavor. Even if early caregivers let the child down or caused emotional or physical harm, or even if the body had other challenges, the capacity to experience sensation and pleasure in the body is a fundamental part of human experience.

These experiences of pleasure become fraught as one grows older, a sad fact that's true for everyone. Bodily pleasure (which we later learn to call "sexuality") inevitably becomes conflicted and complicated, as family, culture, religion, and society impose beliefs on us about pleasure, passion, gender, intimacy, love, beauty, sin, vulnerability, and normalcy.

Adults often find sexual pleasure not as simple, straightforward, or accessible as they had once experienced or hoped. They secretly tell themselves there's something wrong – that they're broken, or their partner's broken, or their relationship is broken, or their childhood was broken. Or, that age or sexual orientation or fantasies or desires make one broken.

Sexuality is complex and multilayered, constantly shifting and evolving. It exists on a fluid continuum of behavior, fantasy, and attraction. We're not fixed in our gender identity and expression; we experience paradox and ambiguity in our sexuality. We can love someone deeply yet not sexually desire that person. We can yearn for a committed relationship, but rule someone out as a potential partner simply because of a physical feature. We can feel aroused by someone, yet not allow ourselves the vulnerability of having an orgasm with that person. In addition, we all are intersectional beings interweaving multiple narratives from our gender, racial, ethnic, and class experiences. Acknowledging all of these complexities within ourselves is at the heart of understanding sexuality, and NRST provides a helpful process for doing so.

The Theoretical Roots of Narrative Relational Sex Therapy

My clinical approach is profoundly influenced by Michael White, an Australian family therapist who developed (with David Epston) Narrative Therapy, which argues that the stories people tell themselves – if not acknowledged and revised – powerfully shape their experiences. In narrative therapy, it is not the person (or couple) who is problematic, it is the story they are telling themselves.

When I first learned about Michel White's work I'd already completed my graduate studies where I attempted to integrate psychoanalytic theory, sexology, and sex research. During graduate school in the 1980s, the importance of sexuality as it relates to psychological development was well established with the work of Freud (1905), which emphasized the role of sexual impulses, drives, and wishes in intra-psychic life. Object relations theorists widened the frame by conceptualizing the interpersonal development of sexuality emphasizing the influence of early childhood relationships (Kernberg, 1995; McDougall, 1995; Person, 1988; Stoller, 1985). Though intellectually robust, some parts of psychoanalytic thinking about sexuality and gender came under fire and were transformed by feminist and queer theorists beginning in the late 1980s, leading to a groundswell of psychoanalytic thinking to date that illuminates the landscape of unconscious processes as they relate to socio-cultural experiences such as gender, sexual orientation, gender identity, race/ethnicity, and class.

An alternative to psychoanalytic discourse on sexuality during my graduate school years was scripting theory, a social constructionist perspective of sexuality developed by sociologists John Gagnon and William Simon (Gagnon & Simon, 1973; Simon & Gagnon, 1986) that explained how cultural and social forces not only give meaning to different sexual behaviors and experiences, but also shape and guide the expression of sexuality, a major departure from essentialist biomedical understandings of sexuality at the time. Though the idea of a script may sound formulaic, elucidating the who, what, where, when, and why of sexual behavior, Gagnon and Simon emphasized the unique scripting of everyday life, the dramatic, performed, improvised experience for each individual. Far from being anti-psychoanalytic, scripting theory described three levels of influence: cultural, interpersonal, and intra-psychic.

In his book *Sexual Excitement* (1979), psychoanalyst Robert Stoller gives tribute to anthropology and sociology in helping him understand the nature of sexual excitement. He states that:

> Gagnon and Simon look at scripts that people create in their minds in order to get excited. To their ideas I would add that conscious scripting, although an essential piece for a theory, serves mainly as the vehicle that carries underlying dynamics, not so much as a force that in itself creates excitement.
>
> (p. 24)

The identification of both conscious scripts and unconscious narratives is part of the NRST process.

Even though Gagnon and Simon's work is not referenced by Michael White (he instead references the work of French philosopher Michel Foucault), I often thought when I encountered White's work after graduate school that if Gagnon and Simon became psychotherapists they would practice Narrative Therapy. Perhaps White didn't reference sexual scripting theory because he did not focus his work on sexuality, per se. Rather, much of his work, like Foucault's, focused on how cultural systems of power create discourses that people internalize as problems about themselves. Applying White's (2007) commitment to identifying the pathologizing internalized narratives about self or others, creating "externalizing conversations in which the problem becomes the problem" (p. 26) to sexuality, combined with contributions from psychoanalysis and sexology, is how NRST developed.

How NRST Starts: A Look at the Opening of a First Session

When people come into therapy, I use the narrative approach immediately. I've found that it often shifts a client's sense of being broken or dysfunctional fairly quickly.

As clients tell me the "presenting problem" (narrative), their "truth" about how one, the other, or both are the problem, I begin to gather information thinking about the narratives contained in the "problem."

I ask questions that begin to deconstruct the problem, for example, when a couple says,

"We don't have sex anymore."

I ask,

"What do you mean by sex?"
"What aren't you doing anymore that you miss?"
"Why is it upsetting to you?"
"Why are you coming for help now?"

These questions help me begin to deconstruct the "problem," to identify narratives about self and other, and to identify parts of what they are doing together that are being discounted because of our predominant cultural narrative of sex (genital contact leading to orgasm).

We develop our narratives throughout our lives and, as we'll see, they can take on very rigid and negative forms. These narratives often then create our actual experiences. How we view ourselves creates our reality, both in and out of the bedroom.

Michael White's work has helped me identify what narratives people bring to therapy and how they can be shifted. Perhaps a mother bought a little girl a new skirt and the dad said, "You look like a tramp, go change your clothes." I've worked with people in their sixties who can remember being told things like that when they were young children. In this case such comments start to create one's narrative (influenced by familial and cultural forces) about displaying sexiness as a girl: "I shouldn't feel good about my body/sexiness" or "I shouldn't display my body/sexiness."

When my clients identify these stories, they may have to work through a great deal of anger or shame or regret or grief with the realization that they've lived much of their lives repressing or avoiding the expression of their sexuality.

This approach isn't an easy sell to clients. Most people are unaware that their deepest obstacles to sexual satisfaction are what they're thinking rather than what they're doing. They ruminate endlessly about how their bodies are unattractive, or that they're sexually awkward, or that their partner is too fat or old or obnoxious for passion to reemerge. Whether these beliefs are accurate or not, the important thing is that they're only the conscious part of the story. Most of the tale remains unconscious and is often deeply painful.

But first, taking clients through an NRST process requires that the therapist's own narratives about what healthy sex is and how change happens need to be transformed.

A Therapist's Path to Narrative Relational Sex Therapy

Unlearning false narratives is as important for therapists as it is for clients. When I teach NRST to therapists around the world, the most consistent feedback I receive is that my work has fundamentally changed the way they always thought about sex, especially the "sacred cows" of desire and orgasm.

When I was first trained by psychoanalysts many years ago, I was taught that all sexual problems stemmed from unconscious conflicts. Once the client had insight into those conflicts, sex would change for the better (greater frequency, more enjoyment, less anxiety, etc.). When that didn't happen, I told myself a story: "The theory is right, so the client must be irrevocably broken."

When I trained in couple and family systems therapy, I learned that all sexual problems had to do with relational problems – buried anger about an affair, poor communication, or emotional disconnection. I was taught that the real issue was *not* sex; a couple's problems were only a symptom of underlying relational problems. Once those problems were rooted out, the sex would improve on its own. When that didn't happen, I told myself: "The theory is right, so the couple must be broken."

When I trained as a sex therapist I learned the Masters and Johnson model, which said that sexual response followed a linear progression from excitement, to plateau, to orgasm, to resolution. Psychoanalyst Helen Singer Kaplan modified this linear model: starting with desire, moving to arousal, and ending in orgasm. The Kaplan model was the one most sex therapists, including myself, were taught. Sexual desire was believed to be a biological drive, like hunger and thirst. You either felt it or you didn't. If desire couldn't be brought back through touch exercises and other behavioral techniques, I told myself, "The theory is right, so the client must be broken."

The point is that therapists have greatly contributed to the harmful narratives that people tell themselves. For years, I had my secret narrative: "Something must be wrong with me as a sex therapist because my clients are still broken!" I was unaware that I had been trained to view sex, which is a complex and multidimensional process, as a fixed, linear, and one-dimensional experience. The NRST method frees us from this imprisonment.

As my thinking and therapeutic techniques evolved over the years, I stopped approaching sex therapy as a technician who could "repair" the "broken" couple, or "fix" the "broken" individual, or get the malfunctioning body parts back to work with medical intervention or behavioral techniques. Likewise, I no longer believed that mere cognitive understanding of erotic desires would change behaviors in the bedroom, although those insights are important. And I no longer had confidence that plumbing the depths of the unconscious for early childhood traumas through psychoanalysis would necessarily bring back desire into a dormant relationship. Nor would desire return by merely teaching someone to communicate and empathize with a partner through couple exercises.

While all of these techniques can help improve a couple's sex life, I found in my practice that such improvement occurs more reliably and dramatically when I helped clients explore family and relational sexual histories dating back to childhood and beyond. I turned my attention to the client's conscious and unconscious sexual history – how sexuality had played out in specific ways in his/her/their life – because that history and its associated narratives are present every time someone has sex.

Sex is usually good at the start of a relationship, but when partners become more familiar with and committed to each other, relational narratives kick in unconsciously. This is why desire too often diminishes in long-term relationships. It's not simply that couples lose the novelty; rather, our conscious and unconscious narratives come into play. As I often tell my clients:

"All sex is group sex. You're in bed with your partner, your/his/hers/their family dynamics, intergenerational traumas, body image, religious upbringing, gender/sexual identity/race/class experiences, on and on. It's crowded in bed!"

The Structure of the Book

This book, divided into two parts, will help therapists unpack clients' sexual lives by describing the theoretical frames and techniques of NRST and how it can be applied to complex sexual issues. The first part will focus on the foundations of NRST.

Chapter 1 looks at one of the central premises guiding my practice – that sex is possible without desire. Too often we've been trained to believe that sex is hopeless without it, but I have found that to be one of the most limiting beliefs in the lives of couples. Instead, newer models based on sound research have shown that satisfying sex doesn't have to begin with desire or end in orgasm. Quite often desire emerges *after* sex starts (Basson, 2001). I introduce clients to the notion of *willingness* (an idea that I gratefully credit to sex therapist JoAnn Loulan, 1984) – that it's possible to initiate and enjoy sex without desire, and the more couples do so, the more their relationship will flourish.

Chapter 2 looks at how the NRST approach goes beyond traditional linear models of sex (desire-arousal-orgasm) to include an expansive variety of sexual motivations, starting points, and ending points. The beauty of this approach is that we can disrupt confining narratives about desire, arousal, and sexual satisfaction, and help clients find their own unique timing and flow to achieve greater pleasure and connection.

Three Main Tools

Starting in Chapter 3, I describe three main tools I use to illuminate the wide range of histories, preferences, and conflicts that clients bring into psychotherapy – the relational sexual history, the sexual menu, and mindful narrative touch. These tools have a common goal: to bring to light and transform clients' troublesome conscious and unconscious sexual narratives so they no longer hinder sexual experience.

The first tool, the in-depth relational sexual history, is the heart of my approach and is described in Chapter 3. Without learning how sexuality had been encountered, expressed, and most importantly, the meaning made of such experiences, starting with the client's earliest memories, you can't help that person achieve liberation from unhealthy beliefs and patterns. The sexual history reveals traumatic sexual and emotional experiences in someone's past. It uncovers challenges with intimacy and attachment wounds. It explores issues of privacy and secrecy, and the difference between the two. It examines how gender identity/expression, sexual orientation, race, skin color, body type, religion, and other social contextual variables were experienced. It identifies pleasures and joys that provide sexual resilience in a client's life. In short, the sexual history, discovered through a series of individual therapeutic conversations about one's sexual journey, provides a "blueprint" for how one's unique sexual narratives evolved, beginning with the question:

"What is your earliest memory of sexuality?"

In Chapter 4 I describe the sexual menu, a creative and playful way to help clients articulate to themselves and their partners what they like and want sexually. Too often, couples never discuss what they enjoy sensually and erot-ically. What are partners willing to try, receive, or share? What are they will-ing to discover together as non-judgmental experimenters? This reinforces, in tangible fashion, the concept of willingness in helping to reinvigorate a sexual life.

The sexual menu challenges the assumption that sex must be genital and orgasmic to "count." It deconstructs sex and equalizes the erotic playing field to include non-genital sexual activity, such as touching, kissing, hugging, massaging, bathing, role-playing, playtoys, sexy talk, reading or viewing erotica, or flirting, to name a few. Clients can tailor the menu to their needs individually and as a couple.

Based on the pioneering contributions of Masters and Johnson (1966) to the field of sex therapy, the relationship between mindfulness and touch, or sensate focus, has been expanded upon in recent years (Brotto, 2018; Iasenza, 2010, 2016; McCarthy & Wald, 2013; Weiner & Avery-Clark, 2017). Our inner narratives fly through our minds at lightning speed, inter-rupting our desire, curiosity, arousal, and fantasy lives without us even real-izing it. I often tell my clients:

"When it comes to sex, our minds are not our friends."

Chapter 5, therefore, provides a detailed description of how to integrate my third main tool – mindful narrative touch – into a sex therapy treat-ment plan. I describe how I teach clients mindfulness techniques to observe and release thoughts so they may be more present during erotic encounters with self and others. If some thoughts contain particularly stubborn disrup-tive narratives, say those related to childhood abuse, these often cannot be released so easily, needing to be processed more in therapy. Mindfulness helps clients access the intensity and immediacy of sexual experiences and diminishes the power of narratives that disrupt pleasure, connection, and sexual satisfaction. With practice, clients develop a capacity for presence, enabling them to fully be in an experience, no matter what is going on cog-nitively, physically, or emotionally.

In Part 2 of *Transforming Sexual Narratives*, I look at how the NRST approach can be applied to challenging and complex sexual issues faced by couples and individuals.

Chapter 6 looks at how sex can be a complex, or "queer," experience for everyone at one time or another, even for asexual clients who often need support in identifying and expressing a sexual orientation that deemphasizes sexual attraction. By "queer" I mean that sex can be unruly, ecstatic, disturbing, confusing, and changeable over one's lifetime. Sex is highly complex, defying easy generalization, categorization, and explanation. Our sexual and gender experiences are often fluid and multidimensional consciously and unconsciously. We all confront incongruities and paradoxes in our behaviors, attractions, thoughts, feelings, dreams, fantasies, and sensations. This chapter will help therapists address these complexities, normalizing the awkwardness they often feel in working with clients who challenge cherished beliefs and assumptions about sexuality and gender.

I discuss how both clients and therapists need to expect and tolerate "queer moments" in relation to sexuality — when we feel perplexed, off balance, or uncomfortable. It's especially important that therapists become tolerant, or even curious, about these moments so they can non-judgmentally manage and learn from moments when triggered or dysregulated. How do both client and therapist deal with feelings of disgust, arousal, shame, confusion, or shock in relation to sexual material?

Chapter 7 takes a clinical look at consensual non-monogamy and polyamory. Poly people believe it's possible (and healthy) to love more than one person and to maintain multiple love/sexual relationships. When it works, it can produce the perfect brain chemistry blend: simultaneous access to both the attraction and attachment phases of romantic love. But helping clients navigate such relationships isn't always easy given the paucity of non-pathologizing psychological theory on the topic. I'll offer a theoretical frame and case material that can help therapists work with this complex issue.

Chapter 8 examines issues about kink, which can include (but isn't limited to) such sexual preferences as spanking, whipping, master/slave, and bondage, or fetishes involving stockings, feet, or leather. Most therapists have been trained to view such preferences/activities as unhealthy or harmful. As a result, many members of the kink community are leery about psychotherapy in much the same way that gay and trans people were in the past. In some discrepant kink couples, where one is into kink and the other is into "vanilla" sex, the kink partner may blame him/her/themself for their sexual problems and/or the partner may do so. It is important that the therapist hold a neutral space for the couple to examine their dynamics about kink.

I view kink in a similar way that I view all sexual preferences involving consenting adults. I look at the quality of relationships in a client's life, not the content of sexual fantasies or preferences, per se. Both kink and vanilla sex relationships have equal potential to be healthy or unhealthy. Relationship "health" isn't based on particular sexual preferences or practices of the partners, but rather the particular relationship experiences (and associated narratives) that create distress in the present.

I take a detailed account of how and when kink emerged in a client's sexual history, not for the purpose of identifying how the present kink represents or perpetuates harmful patterns from the past, but instead to determine if/how negative, shameful narratives about kink affected the development of a fully integrated sexual life. It's important that therapists refrain from pathologizing kink even if in some cases a client is distressed by their kink preferences. In those cases, the client could be struggling with internalized kink negativity. The best of NRST work could be utilized by identifying the earliest memories of kink desire and what narratives were created that contribute to the distress a client is experiencing in the present.

Chapter 9 looks at the phenomenon of emotional sadism in couples. While even the best marriages or relationships have conflict, emotional sadism goes far beyond the normal aggression or states of hatred that most people experience. Couple therapist David Schnarch (1991) coined the term "normal marital sadism" as an attempt to normalize sadistic impulses that are often expressed as selfishness and self-interest in couple sexual relations. This chapter will take emotional sadism one step further to describe the pernicious effects of enduring patterns of sadistic malevolence in some couples.

Unlike normal marital difficulty, emotional sadism becomes a way of being for some couples – an entrenched, unconscious, co-created dynamic of emotional sadism/masochism that becomes the only way they can relate and feel connected. It involves getting pleasure from emotionally harming someone, a pattern that is often related to childhood attachments that are reenacted in the present relationship. When sex is a presenting problem, these couples are often clueless about how their co-creation of a negative erotic environment contributes to their sexless relationship. Therapists often feel particularly challenged, or even defeated, by these couples since partners often collude to subvert the therapist's attempts to disrupt enmeshed relational patterns (Willi, 1977). I will show through NRST case histories how therapists can help clients understand, illuminate, and shift this behavior, instead of surrendering to it.

Chapter 10 is about the empowerment of connecting with and reclaiming one's sexual birthright, whether one is in a relationship or single. Everyone is a sexual being, including people who don't have a partner. I introduce the concept of intentional pleasure and the usefulness of bringing willingness into a client's solo sex life. When desire wanes for a single person, they might feel they've entirely lost their sexuality. While this chapter is primarily for singles, it's important to remember that couples contain two individuals who, unless they are enmeshed in giving up sexual agency and personal power, can benefit from lifelong individual sexual development. With singles as well as couples, willingness is a powerful cognitive skill. It enables the clients to have a robust and continuous erotic life whether or not they experience desire or are in a relationship. Chapter 10 shows how both singles and coupled partners can explore intentional pleasure to maintain more satisfying erotic lives.

The Promise of Narrative Relational Sex Therapy

Transforming Sexual Narratives will help therapists access a deeper and richer understanding of what their clients' particular sexual problems really represent. It provides them with the concepts and tools to help clients rewrite their sexual narratives to make their sex lives easier and more rewarding. Sexual problems mirror the difficulties of one's past. Consequently, they provide an opportunity for personal growth and healing. By transforming how we view sexuality, we can learn how to be with others and ourselves in a more present, open, and expansive way.

Our clients are not "the broken ones" who can never be fixed, as I once mistakenly believed. Everyone can have a more satisfying erotic life. *Transforming Sexual Narratives* provides the theory and practice needed to make that possible. And as your clients learn to apply the NRST process, it's very likely that they will transform other narratives as well, leading to more authentic and satisfying work lives, friendships, and family relationships.

For the vast majority of people, destructive sexual narratives remain invisible and unexamined. We must address the roots of the dilemma to help bring these narratives into the light to transform and utilize them. Without learning how to do so, we can't help our clients (and ourselves, as therapists) become liberated from destructive sexual narratives. *Transforming Sexual Narratives* gives you the theories and the tools to help you and your clients along that journey.

PART 1

THE FOUNDATIONS OF NARRATIVE
RELATIONAL SEX THERAPY (NRST)

CHAPTER 1

✳

SEX IS POSSIBLE WITHOUT DESIRE

Justin and Kris, a strikingly attractive couple in their early forties, sat across from me in my office for their first therapy appointment. Married for ten years, they had once been passionate partners, but that part of their lives was now history.

"We haven't made love in over a year," Kris told me, her voice barely audible.

Justin, occupying the far end of the couch, stared miserably at the rug. "I don't have a clue about where to go with this," he finally said, shrugging his shoulders in resignation.

I begin the first session with couples by asking them to describe what attracted them to each other, as a way to explore with partners what they once shared – and may be able to revive. Or, sometimes couples forget that their initial attraction was not sexual or physical, but years later want to experience something they never had. In Kris and Justin's case, physical attraction was strong from the beginning.

"We met online and started exchanging these playful, sexy messages," said Kris, blushing a little.

"When we finally got together in person at a local bar, it was lust at first sight," Justin chimed in.

Kris nodded. "I loved his tall, lean body and his gorgeous green eyes." She stole a look at her husband.

"And I was wowed by the way Kris approached me," said Justin. "She radiated this amazing mix of confidence and flirtation."

"We talked about everything and laughed for hours," Kris added.

"Then I drove her home," Justin said. "But before we even made it to her block, we pulled the car over." On a side street they made love, hard and fast, and never looked back, dating exclusively within weeks and marrying six months later.

"You started off with a lot of desire," I said. "Then what happened?"

"In the early years, our sexual attraction was pretty intense and constant," Kris said.

"Everything was easy," Justin added. "We bought a house and decorated it together. We agreed that we didn't want kids, and we both loved our work." Kris was an attorney for a prominent firm, while Justin was a high school guidance counselor.

"And then?" I asked.

"Well, at first I didn't notice that our sex life had changed," said Justin. "Then I began to see that I was the one who was always initiating. We still had sex with orgasms, but Kris seemed less into it."

"I felt I was pushing myself to enjoy the experience," admitted Kris. "My desire just wasn't there."

At this, Justin's lips tightened. "In my worst moments, I've wondered if she's been having an affair," he said bitterly. "She works crazy hours during the week and avoids me on the weekends." He took a deep breath, but his brow remained deeply furrowed. "I'll be honest – at this point I don't much care whether we have sex or not."

"I love him," Kris broke in, "and I still think he's the most attractive guy I know. But I can't believe that Justin doesn't appreciate how hard I work at the firm or understand my need for some alone time on weekends," she said. Her arms were folded across her chest. "I feel pretty close to hopeless. I mean, how can we have sex if we don't want each other?"

After confirming that neither of them had been talking directly to each other about sexual issues, I wasn't surprised to hear that they were arguing constantly, about everything from spending habits to the correct placement of food in the refrigerator. They had been referred by the gynecologist Kris had consulted for her "desire problem." As they sat with me now, both reported feeling turned off, pissed off, and helpless to make a change.

Humans have been having sex throughout history. Yet, despite the vast accumulation of art, music, poetry, and literature on the subject, the advice passed down from parent to child, the *Kama Sutra*, the porn industry, magazine articles that "de-mystify" orgasms and erogenous zones, sex chat rooms, and on and on, couples of all sexual orientations still encounter the same old problems in the bedroom. The initial passion wanes, the partners blame themselves or the other partner, and conflict gets expressed both inside and outside of the bedroom. Disappointment, bitterness, disconnection, or open hostility often follow. How could something that was once satisfying become so fraught with awkwardness and tension?

To address this problem, most therapists focus on fostering good communication skills, come up with more constructive options to resolve conflict, and help partners learn to negotiate and compromise. For several decades these techniques have been thought to improve the erotic environment for a couple, and they sometimes do.

But where else can we turn for answers? In my practice as a psychodynamically oriented sex therapist, I have found that couples' erotic lives improve reliably and dramatically when I help them identify and transform unconscious internalized narratives derived from family and other relationship histories.

In addition to individual unconscious narratives that were formulated in childhood, we are all exposed to social scripts (Gagnon & Simon, 1973; Laws & Schwartz, 1977) that shape us from an early age – homophobia, transphobia, sexism, racism, classism, and all the other "isms."

Psychoanalytic theory is based on the assumption that all adult romantic relationships have their roots in infancy and childhood. From the moment children are born, they relate to objects (people, caregivers) around them and start internalizing, or introjecting, their influence. For example: you cry, mommy (caregiver) feeds you, and you get the message that the world is a caring place. If you have a caregiver who ignores your screaming, you learn that no one is coming to help you with your needs. We carry our internalized messages with us for the rest of our lives. Imago therapy, which became popular in the 1990s with Harville Hendrix's book *Getting the Love You Want*, focuses on how partners' interactions are based on internalizations from their earliest caregivers' relationships with them – typically, the parent-child dyad.

Theorists at the Tavistock Institute of Human Relations in London went beyond the parent-child dyad to examine the "internalized parental couple," a concept associated with the Object Relations branch of psychoanalysis. Toddlers and young children internalize their first experience of a parental couple (which could also be a single parent's relationship to an absent spouse/partner – two parents don't have to be physically present). In this vein, I have found it to be remarkably helpful to ask couples to explore their first models of romantic relationship. Awareness of the parental dyad is often a child's first experience of feeling excluded, leading to his or her first experience of feeling jealous and competitive. I help clients see what they might unconsciously be replicating in their adult relationships, in patterns that can be both constructive and destructive.

G.R. DiCeglie, in his paper "From the Internal Parental Couple to the Marital Relationship" (1995), emphasized that the experience of our parents' relationship influences how we conduct adult relationships, saying that in the best of all worlds we can have and want, desire and identify with, both members of the parental couple in a fluid way. This enables us to experience the greatest degree of flexibility and richness in adult love relationships. When one or both parents relate dysfunctionally with the child and/or each other, the child's ability to fluidly move amongst all possible internal parental object relations is hindered. These hindrances emerge later in adult love relations as sexual shutdowns, anxieties, or defenses. One of my goals is to help couples reveal and work through the unconscious conflicts underlying their sexual difficulties.

Even though our romantic and sexual relationships may appear quite different from our parents', psychoanalysts believe that none of us, no matter what our sexual orientation or gender identity, escapes the messages (good and bad) from childhood. In my experience, inquiring about the internalized parental couple moves my clients' work to a deeper level beyond the present relationship, freeing them from confusing sexual patterns that often involve the loss of desire (Iasenza, 2006).

The Case of Bob and Carl

Like Justin and Kris, Bob and Carl were experiencing problems with sexual connection. Both in their forties, they came to see me for therapy because both reported loss of sexual desire, taking turns refusing offers of sex during their five-year relationship. Their sexual histories contained ample evidence of enjoyable sexual experiences, both partnered and solo. They presented as a peer marriage (Schwartz, 1994) – intellectually, emotionally, and socially well-matched. They bought and furnished beautiful homes in Manhattan and outside the city. Carl's parents, who lived near them, welcomed Bob as their son-in-law. The men enjoyed a rich social network of colleagues, friends, and family, and were out to everyone as an openly gay couple.

Bob grew up in a Southern Baptist family. Both of his parents abused alcohol, and his father was physically and verbally abusive. Bob became aware of his sexual and romantic feelings for boys very early, but knew that his physical and mental survival depended on secrecy and silence because of his parents' strict religious beliefs and his father's obsession with hyper-masculinity about himself and his two sons. Bob didn't have much of a social life, and his sexual explorations were confined to masturbation (fantasizing only about boys) throughout his teen years.

As Bob and his brother entered adolescence, his father's abuse and neglect of his mother intensified, and she regularly turned to her teenage sons for company and comfort. Bob remembers with disgust and anger her controlling rituals, demanding that he and his brother kiss her on the lips before leaving the house or hug her tightly before they retired at night. Bob saved himself by excelling in academics and leaving home for college. He decided to come out to his parents at the end of his senior year of high school, only to have his father disown him and refuse to pay for college. He never wanted to meet any of Bob's boyfriends. Bob's mother, afraid to defy her husband, silently went along with him.

Carl and his sister were raised in a comfortable, middle-class New York family with supportive and attentive parents who often praised him. His father and mother were highly successful and well-known in their fields, and they encouraged Carl and his sister to pursue their unique talents. Carl had traveled throughout Europe by the time he was a teenager and took private music and language lessons. His parents were very polite with each other and enjoyed focusing on their children's achievements. He could hardly remember them fighting. His seemed like the perfect family.

Carl was a straight-A student and president of the debate club, as achievement was highly valued in his family. He believed his parents would probably react well to the news that he was gay because many of their friends were openly gay and lesbian, but he carried a deep concern about not measuring up to their expectations; he suspected that their outward politeness might hide feelings of disappointment.

As a slightly built, non-athletic boy, Carl was taunted and bullied so badly by boys in the locker room that he avoided the showers and dressed as quickly as he could whenever "hey faggot" started getting thrown around. He never reported these shaming experiences to anyone, including his parents. He openly dated girls and secretly dated boys throughout his early teen years, until he fell in love at age fifteen with a boy. By senior year the pressure of the secrecy was too much for Carl's boyfriend, who abruptly announced one day that he was "going straight."

Carl was devastated because he thought he would spend the rest of his life with his boyfriend. He suffered in silence, never letting on to his parents how wounded he was. He didn't come out to them until after college, when his mother asked why he was so distant and didn't bring friends home to meet the family. Both parents were supportive when he came out, but in the midst of their acceptance Carl mostly felt grief about the many years he had suffered in loneliness and secrecy in his family.

As Bob and Carl shared their histories in therapy, they began to realize how much they were replicating key family dynamics with each other. Saying no to sex was protective for both of them. Bob needed to feel some control after so much violent and inappropriate behavior from both parents, and Carl wanted to protect himself from the abandonment he experienced with his first boyfriend and that he feared from his parents. Neither had experienced parental couples who expressed anger in constructive ways, and each felt pulled into the parental triangle to contain their parents' conflicts.

Once some of their unconscious motivations about saying no to sex were revealed, we began the work of creating an erotic environment in which they could explore, expand, and enjoy their sexual potential with or without sexual desire. Having good sex often mobilizes guilt and anxiety about boundary maintenance, comfort with intimacy, body image, religious and family attitudes about sex, and feelings of worthiness. The family, relationship, and sexual histories of lesbian women and gay men often can contain additional sources of sexual guilt, anxiety, and shame due to societal and internalized homophobia.

Sex therapy helped Bob and Carl begin to break the silences and secrets that characterized their sexual life with each other. As they shared fantasies and wishes – first in sessions and then at home – they created a safe space to overcome sexual shame and express their particular sexual needs. Bob transformed his narrative that attachment involves harm by working through his fear and anger about the abuse in his family, and Carl transformed his narrative that love leads to abandonment by grieving the loss of his teenage boyfriend, permitting himself to trust "putting all his eggs in one basket."

Contemporary psychoanalysts (Chodorow, 1994; Dimen, 2014; Harris, 2005) posit that unconscious life doesn't strictly adhere to traditional gender roles. We internalize all gendered parts – female and male, masculine and feminine, active and passive. We internalize them whether we have two dads, two moms, a single parent, a trans parent, or even an absent parent. Recent clinical writing (Corbett, 2009) explores how some children who were created with the help of sperm donors still have a relationship to that anonymous parent in dreams and fantasy, which contributes to their internalized parental couple dynamics. Past and present partners of single parents can play a role in child development, as well as how the single parent relates to him/her/themself and the world as an erotic being. Even if people's parents divorced at a very young age, they still internalized narratives about what was going on before and during the split, as well as how formerly married parents related afterward. Clients who lost a parent to illness or accident can form an internalized imaginary parental couple even when one parent is missing. It doesn't matter what the anatomical or socially constructed gender is of parents or the particular family configuration (biological children, adopted children, foster children). All children internalize messages about love, power, danger, and safety from early caregiving relationships and from witnessing the intimacy (or the absence thereof) between early caregivers.

The Case of Sara and Joan

Another powerful example of internalized narratives and loss of sexual desire is the case of Sara and Joan, a couple in their forties who were sadly considering ending their relationship. For the past ten years they had great fun together, felt like soulmates, were intellectually and politically in sync, yet were at their wits' end to find a way to work out their sexual problems. They each reported low levels of desire and had sporadic sex during the previous five years. They attributed the change in sexual frequency to an acute depression that Sara experienced when she lost an important job, but no improvement followed when the depression lifted.

As we reviewed their sexual history, it turned out that even though they had sex regularly during the first decade, the quality of their sex seemed more defensive than deeply intimate. As with Bob and Carl, their family histories gave us some understanding as to why. Sara grew up in an alcoholic family; her father's drinking led to job losses and her mother was clinically depressed. Sara took care of her four younger siblings and worried about her mother's suicidal threats, which she made every few weeks. For Sara, experiencing a deeper sexual intimacy with Joan (a "heart-opening sexuality," as she called it) felt too risky, especially since Joan had revealed how attracted she was to other women. Sara felt if she lost Joan she'd lose herself, which is the same way she felt about her suicidal mother.

Joan grew up witnessing her mother and father fighting about her father's infidelities. She felt angry with her father and sad for her mother. She remembered deciding early on that she would never put herself in her mother's position, and coped with the strife at home by getting involved at school and dating girls early on. She was very attractive and experienced power in getting girls interested in her. When she met Sara, she enjoyed seducing her. She also came to realize that her flirtations with other women was her way of making doubly sure she would never be in her mother's situation.

Once we discussed each of their internalized parental couples, the partners stopped personalizing the other's behavior. Realizing that the source of the problem existed before they met, they relaxed a bit and stopped blaming themselves or each other: this created space for each partner to take a more objective (less defensive) look at her contribution to the couple dynamics.

Therapy helped Joan and Sara realize how their defensive feelings about sexuality protected them from experiencing the vulnerabilities associated with their parents. As they transformed the narratives associated with their childhood challenges, they were able to revive their sexual life by using willingness as an entryway to sexual connection. Sara could open herself emotionally to Joan when they had sex, and Joan was able to give up her flirtations and imagined affairs with other women to let Sara be her one and only. Their sexual crisis helped them create a safe erotic space where they could be more passionately connected than ever before.

The assumption that psychoanalysis only uncovers problems is mistaken. A thorough exploration of early life often leads to a discovery of hidden and untapped resources and resiliency. Clients discover memories of parents, or other significant couples, who were loving, romantic, and had fun with each other; accessing these memories can help in adult relationships. Some clients realize how supportive sex education from parents or other adults helps them in their current relationships. Or, someone who experienced childhood abuse may be thus enabled to bring compassion to a partner's struggles with sexual shame.

Clients who come from families where parents never touched or kissed can learn to be affectionate with their partners by understanding that their propensity to avoid physical intimacy was a learned behavior associated with narratives that, if they choose, can be transformed. What the cases of Bob and Carl and Sara and Joan illustrate is that identifying and transforming sexual narratives associated with childhood wounds, including those associated with the parental couple, removes an important barrier to sexual connection. When combined with the offer of new narratives of the sexual response cycle – namely, normalizing beginning sex with willingness instead of desire – couples may move from reenactment of childhood patterns to co-creating sexual connection in adulthood.

The Notion of Willingness

Let's return to the case of Kris and Justin, the once-passionate couple who hadn't had sex in a year. Like most people, they believed that desire was necessary to start a sexual encounter. Since neither felt desire, they thought they were at a dead end. I challenged this belief in the first session.

"It sounds like you both believe that sex must begin with desire," I said. "But there are newer models, based on good research, showing that satisfying sex doesn't have to begin with desire or end in orgasm. And for some people, desire emerges *after* sex starts."

Kris looked intrigued.

"One crucial element," I continued, "is the notion of willingness. You can initiate sex not because you feel horny, but because you trust that once you get started you'll begin to enjoy it. And the more you enjoy it, the more your relationship will flourish."

Now, both Kris and Justin looked interested.

"Can you imagine trying willingness as a way to work toward sexual connection?" I asked.

They looked at each other for a moment, and then nodded. "We've got nothing to lose."

Once Kris and Justin had confirmed their willingness to reestablish a sexual connection (with or without desire), I introduced the most crucial element of our work together. "In order to work more deeply on your issues, we need to gather information on your family, sexual, and relationship histories," I began. "That will help us to understand how each of you became sexual beings and how your sexual stories are influencing your sex life now."

To accomplish this, I told them I'd need to meet with each of them individually for three to five sessions. This kind of in-depth relational history-taking is a powerful experience for sexually stuck partners. For the therapist, it's an opportunity to create a safe, non-judgmental space within which clients can tell their sexual stories. For many people this experience is transformative in itself, as it's usually the first time they've examined, thought about, and shared their sexual development with another person, let alone their partner.

Discovering the Client's Sexual History

After conducting the sexual history with Kris (how I conduct the history will be explained in detail in Chapter 3), I discovered that her father abruptly abandoned the family when she was three years old, leaving her terrified of closeness and dependency. Her mother was chronically depressed, suffering more serious bouts after Kris's father left. By the time she was ten years old, Kris was cleaning house and buying groceries when her mother was too despondent to get out of bed. Her mother would try to comfort her about her father's abandonment, saying things like, "It wasn't about you, honey.

25

Your father left because of me. All men leave. Don't trust them." What her mother thought were helpful comments instead created a central narrative for Kris: "Love a man and he'll leave you." Based on her history, Kris had plenty of reasons to keep Justin at arm's length.

Sexual shame, guilt, or remorse can have profound and enduring effects on sexuality, and in an individual history session Justin revealed a secret — that a trusted coach had molested him when he was twelve years old. "I'm still ashamed that I let it continue for a whole semester," he said in a near-whisper. "At the time, I wondered what was wrong with me. Why did he pick me? Was I gay?" The silent narrative developed early on that "something is shameful and wrong with me sexually" contributed to Justin's feelings of deficiency later in life.

This was true in Kris's case as well. Perhaps in an attempt to nurture her daughter, her mother kept her company whenever Kris took a bath. "We'd talk a while, and then she'd stare at me and say things like 'You could stand to lose a few pounds' and 'Men like their women to stay attractive,'" Kris told me, fighting tears. For the first time she realized how deeply she had internalized those messages, constructing a narrative that made her self-conscious and self-critical when making love. Her trim body notwithstanding, she harbored a longstanding belief that she was "a fat slob."

How Our Sexual Histories Shape Us

As a client identifies memories containing important sexual and/or emotional experiences, I ask:

"How does that experience affect your sexuality or intimacy now?"

For many individuals, these early experiences — and especially the meaning they make of them — shape the development of their sexual narratives. During the history-taking process I start to reframe clients' experiences, normalize some of them, and offer psycho-education to help them revise those parts of their past that contribute to negative sexual narratives. This key part of the process of Narrative Relational Sex Therapy (NRST), the transforming of negative sexual narratives, will be explored in detail throughout this book.

When Justin told me that his coach had molested him, I took the time to educate him about sexual abuse. "It says more about the perpetrator than it does about the survivor," I said. "It's an abuse of power that has nothing to do with your masculinity or sexual orientation." When I added that it would have been very hard for him to make the abuse public, he realized that his father wouldn't have believed him and might have even ridiculed him. "And my mom wouldn't have intervened, no matter what," he said sadly.

No wonder Justin had stayed silent about the abuse for nearly thirty years. It reflected how invisible he felt in his family, as well as his conviction that "real boys don't get molested" (a common faulty cultural narrative). By the time we finished this exploration, he felt compassion for the young Justin who was preyed upon and had nowhere to turn.

In addition to family, I explore relationship history, including first crushes, significant romantic relationships, and sexual experiences (solo and partnered). I pay special attention to early attachments and role-modeling that shaped the client's beliefs about the body, sex, intimacy, and emotional safety.

Sex and Attachment Theory

Attachment theory (Bowlby, 1988) helps us understand how clients develop styles of attachment (secure, anxious, avoidant) based on childhood relationship experiences. When applied to couples (Johnson, 2004; Johnson, Simakhodskaya, & Moran, 2018), partners may be guided to explore how much they co-create a safe haven or secure base to support emotional and sexual connection, including the expression of desire. I often explore with clients how early attachment experiences currently affect expectations of others, especially one's partner.

Justin, for example, realized how deeply his parental couple dynamics affected his feelings about Kris. His alcoholic father raged at his mother, who silently absorbed her husband's wrath. "When I got to be a teenager, I would sometimes defend her," said Justin, "but that only made my father crazier." So Justin learned to keep his anger to himself.

In our individual session, Justin came to understand how complex his sexual story was. He was involved in a deep struggle to manage familiar feelings of neglect, combined with a fear that "if I asserted my sexual needs, including my sexual desire for her, when Kris seemed uninterested, I'd become a monster" – either aggressive like his father or abusive like his coach. Separately, Kris came to realize how much she was influenced by the narrative "a man will leave you." She worked hard to become a successful, independent career woman who could always take care of herself. "I was sure that, sooner or later, Justin would pack up and go," she said, then hypothesized that the "desire disorder" she presented to her gynecologist was an unconscious, misguided attempt to protect herself from reliving her (and her mother's) emotional history. "If you don't want a man too much," she told me, "you won't be as hurt when he leaves."

As I listened to Justin and Kris, I focused less on the particulars of their histories than on the meanings they made of their experiences. It was becoming clear how their narratives were maintaining their sexual-relational difficulties. As we finished up the individual history sessions, we discussed what parts of their stories they felt comfortable sharing with each other, a crucial step in NRST work. Sooner or later, they would have to confront their struggles with desire together.

Displacing Desire's Major Role in Sexual Activity

Sexual desire has occupied a central place in the psychological-medical-cultural imagination ever since Masters and Johnson's renowned Human Sexual Response Cycle (1966) (excitement, plateau, orgasm, resolution) was replaced by Helen Singer Kaplan's (1979) Triphasic Sexual Response Model (desire, arousal, orgasm). For generations, these models defined the template for what's supposed to be a healthy sexual life for couples, often determining whether they had sex at all. Both models impose a rigid, linear scheme on what's actually a complex, multidimensional relational process. (For a thorough critique of the Human Sexual Response Cycle, see the work of sexologist Leonore Tiefer [1995].)

Most sex therapists, myself included, were trained in a version of the sexual response model, which implies that sexual desire is a biological drive like hunger or thirst. In the early years of my practice, if my clients failed to experience regular and reliable desire, I concluded that they needed medical and/or behavioral interventions, which might include referral for hormone supplements, prescribed date nights, or viewing porn. These methods were supposed to move clients along toward the end-all, be-all goal of orgasm.

The trouble is that for many couples, these kinds of approaches simply don't work. Many couples try hard to resuscitate passion, fail miserably, and conclude that their relationship is hopelessly dysfunctional or broken, when this isn't necessarily the case.

In fact, the absence of desire is not the problem, it is the narrative that desire is a prerequisite for human sexual activity. This one narrative is a recipe for disappointment. For most couples, the initial infatuation phase, during which one's partner is experienced as the most desirable person, inevitably wanes. If it diminishes altogether, many couples either resign themselves to a sexless relationship or split up, hoping to feel desire with a new partner.

My experience is that many couples can rekindle desire, but not as the first order of business. Narrative Relational Sex Therapy (NRST) presents a different way of thinking about sexual challenges related to desire. Rather than focusing on desire at the front end, couples like Justin and Kris can identify and transform their unconscious sexual narratives – cultural, familial, personal, relational, and bodily – that interfere with their capacity to connect sexually. Once partners identify and share core parts of their sexual histories with each other, defenses begin to dissolve, sexual engagement can begin with willingness, bodies can experience sensations or pleasures without a predetermined goal, and desire has a chance to reawaken.

How Can We Have Sex Without Desire?

To help Kris and Justin rekindle their sex lives, I asked them to put desire aside – at least for the moment. Instead, I wanted their permission to share the stories that seemed most central to their current sexual difficulties. To prepare them for this step, I introduced the *narrative integration process*: "I want you to understand that your loss of desire has deep roots, going back to experiences and meanings that existed long before you met each other. Your marriage recreated the early experiences that hurt you. So, with your permission, I'll now share parts of your sexual histories."

Soon Justin began to understand how scary it would be for Kris to put both feet into a relationship, given her father's abandonment. In addition, he was shocked at the messages Kris's mom gave her. "I had no idea that she'd talked to you about men leaving, or her judgment of you as unattractive," he said. "For the record, that's crap. You're *very* attractive."

For her part, Kris was deeply saddened by Justin's story of the sexual abuse he'd endured. She took in how embattled and unworthy he felt in the face of both his father's uncontrollable rage and his coach's horrific betrayal. "You were just a kid," she said softly.

Justin and Kris emerged from these sessions with an understanding of how each of them had unconsciously contributed to their sexless marriage. Listening to each other's intimate stories kindled empathy for their struggles. As compassion began to replace anger, they became ready to begin treatment as allies in the healing process.

The Possibility of Erotic Liberation

At this point, we moved from history-taking to the creation of a sexual menu – a list of enticing sexual activities that partners first generate individually and then as a couple.

In my experience, the sexual history facilitates the sexual menu process by opening up what was once secret and shameful (with the therapist, at first), and inspiring mutual empathy that frees a couple to begin to explore new pathways to pleasure. Thanks to the history-taking process, all of us recognized how tough it was for Justin and Kris to express their needs. Being aware of their private sexual concerns also allowed me to help them move more safely through the menu process. They brainstormed their individual and mutual sexual menus, a process that will be described in detail in Chapter 4.

Next, I had Justin and Kris explore mindful touch, as a way to jumpstart their physical connection. To their enormous credit, Masters and Johnson understood the importance of touch fifty years ago when they devised progressive "sensate focus" exercises in which couples start with non-erotic touch, progress to erotic touch, and finally move to genital sex. (I will describe how mindful touch helped Kris and Justin reconnect sexually in Chapter 5.)

Justin and Kris decided to begin a weekly date that started with individual meditation time, followed by mindful touching, and then one item from their couple sexual menu. Becoming more playful, they wrote down all of their menu items on slips of paper, stuffed them into a hat, and plucked out one per week. They loved how their menu items, some of which included genital contact and others that didn't, freed them from the performance and response anxiety associated with the desire-to-orgasm narrative. Instead, they simply looked forward to their erotic time each week, replacing desire with willingness and discovering that passion was generated by having sex – not the other way around.

Whenever I celebrate a success story like Kris and Justin's, I'm also very aware that not all people are willing or able to do the sometimes harrowing work of facing and revising their sexual narratives. Some partners are too frightened to go into their early years; others are too disheartened by years of sexual "failure" to make the effort. It's our job as therapists to challenge old treatment models that make couples feel broken. We need to let clients know that the greatest barriers to a more satisfying sex life aren't biologically based but are socially taught. Armed with that understanding, they can begin to invent their own approach to a more fulfilling sexual connection, encompassing whatever activities, sensations, and states of being they enjoy. Uncovering sexual narratives – often brimming with pain and need – and sharing them with others makes erotic liberation possible.

Peer Relationships and Sexual Desire

One type of relationship that typically involves desire issues is the peer relationship, defined by sociologist and sexologist Pepper Schwartz (1994) in *Love Between Equals: How Peer Marriage Really Works* as a relationship of "equal companions, a collaboration of love and labor in order to produce profound intimacy and mutual respect" (p. 2). Schwartz first developed the notion of peer relationships in 1983, when she, with co-researcher Philip Blumstein, conducted one of the most comprehensive studies of couples in the United States. The ten-year project consisted of 12,000 questionnaires and 600 interviews of married and co-habitating heterosexual, gay, and lesbian couples.

The researchers found egalitarian qualities to be more common in gay and lesbian relationships because partners didn't have to overcome traditional gender roles, as did heterosexuals, to develop relationships that felt fair and mutually supportive. Since the 1990s, I've been increasingly working with heterosexual couples who have peer relationships, which I credit to a generation of men and women having grown up with feminism. Thus, the importance of working with desire issues in peer relationships is now mainstream.

Peer partners are usually non-conflictual. Each person has equal status and is equally responsible for emotional, economic, and household duties. There is usually intense companionship, as both partners feel the relationship is fair and mutually supportive. Their relationship is deeply satisfying on every level – parenting, financial and domestic collaboration, friendship, intimacy, and communication – but their sexual relations are often infrequent. With all the love, companionship, genuine enjoyment, and pleasure in the relationship, why does this happen?

Some partners in peer relationships feel reconciled to having infrequent sexual activity, as the other satisfying qualities of the relationship take priority over sex. Those couples usually don't seek sex therapy. Others do seek therapy because they want to understand their low sexual desire. For many therapists, this is one of the hardest couple's issues to navigate successfully. It would make sense to hear about low sexual desire among couples who have nasty fights or engage in constant bickering. But Schwartz's research showed otherwise. What is it about a satisfying emotional and intimate connection that inhibits some partners in the bedroom?

One hypothesis is that peer partners feel so connected and fulfilled in other ways that they don't need sex to feel bonded. Another hypothesis is that peer partners' smooth sailing in equal decision-making and relationship management might belie an underlying lack of differentiation that may not interfere with household negotiations but may be quite threatening if an active sexual life reveals serious underlying differences in sexual preferences. A third hypothesis is that peer couples put such great emphasis on equality and equity that they have trouble shifting into bedroom roles, where intentional or unintentional power inequities often make for the most exciting sex. They can't make the transition from romantic sex into the lust and objectification that often fuel sexual intensity. Sex becomes routine, almost too friendly. It lacks the edge of risk-taking and novelty. They can't "use" their partner in the service of pure pleasure because it contradicts their sense of equality and equity.

How are these issues different from those experienced by "traditional" couples where sex can easily become familiar, routine, and at times nonexistent? The difference may not lie in possible underlying reasons for sexual decline, but in how long it might take for the decline to happen. In gay, lesbian, or heterosexual couples with "traditional" unequal power relations, sexual roles are clear making initiation and receptivity more routine, and whether imbued with tremendous desire or not, may help sexuality activity continue longer over time.

Desire, Lust, and Power Relations

Two quotes from psychoanalytic writers exploring the connection between intense sex and the qualities that fuel lust may shed some light on the issue of desire in peer relationships.

In *On the Subjectivity of Lustful States of Mind*, Martin Frommer (2006) writes:

> The ability to lust where one loves is contingent on the capacity to bring otherness of self forward in the context of attachment. The dampening or deadening of desire in long-term relationships may be understood, counter-intuitively, not as a failure of the integration of lust with love but as a breakdown in the normative dissociative processes on which the emergence of lust depends.

(p. 1)

In his book, *Forces of Destiny*, Christopher Bollas (1989) writes:

> Ruthlessness has something to do with a joint loss of consciousness, a thoughtlessness which is incremental to erotic intensity. It is a necessary ruthlessness as both lovers destroy the relationship in order to plunge into reciprocal orgasmic use. Indeed, the destruction of relationship is itself pleasurable and the conversion of relating to using transforms ego libido into increased erotic drive.
>
> (p. 26)

These quotes go to the heart of our contradictions about sexuality. Too much ruthlessness and objectification during sex can lead to degradation or even harm. But too little of either and we have the peer marriage situation: best friends who repress lust and desire. I've had many therapeutic conversations with feminist clients (male, female, and non-binary) about how to distinguish among sexual assertiveness, sexual aggression (desired by both partners), and sexual coercion/violence.

It's a matter of balance. Ruthlessness and objectification have to happen within a context of safety, equality, and respect, not coerciveness. Sex can get out of control and cross boundaries in ways that are unhealthy and even harmful, as we're learning more about in the #MeToo movement. In an abusive relationship, whether heterosexual, gay, or trans, power is misused both in and outside the bedroom, as objectification cuts across sexuality into nonsexual areas as well. Objectification only works within a larger relational context of non-objectification, where there is a great deal of respect and equality already established. Otherwise, one partner is being used or giving in. (For a contemporary discussion of sexual agency versus sexual coercion, see the work of sexologist Meg Kaplan [2018].)

A New Model of Eroticism

Because peer couples are not anchored in hierarchal difference, as is the case with traditional couples, they offer the possibility of a new model of eroticism that's not based on assumed power differences.

Or, to look at it another way: if there are hierarchical differences in a peer relationship, those differences are consciously embraced. Peer couples can learn how to tolerate and develop the fluidity between equality and inequality for the sake of keeping erotic tension alive. They can have conscious equality when it comes to parenting, money, careers, who takes out the garbage, etc. But they also can develop and play with inequality in the bedroom, and deal with whatever discomfort or conflicts may arise as a result. They can become comfortable with using power in a more ruthless way. To be clear, that's not the same as using power incorrectly or harmfully, either inside or outside the bedroom.

Generally speaking, one characteristic of a peer couple is that they are capable of more empathy and understanding than traditional couples. They are often more open to cooperation and teamwork, relational skills that form a solid foundation for sexual experimentation. Traditional couples tend to have more challenges with communication and empathy.

The therapist's goal is to help the traditional couple become a little bit more like the peer couple in terms of emotional skills and intelligence, which can serve as a foundation for better sexual teamwork. The therapist may also help the peer couple become more like a traditional couple, not in giving up their equality outside the bedroom, but rather "intra-psychically," to allow for the inequality that can fuel the expression of desire.

How do they create this new narrative? It often requires a great deal of help from me. One partner might say, "I don't want to dominate him or him to dominate me. That doesn't fit with how we feel about each other. Then we're not really equal."

And I might respond, "Well, how about the equality being one level up?" In other words, the real equality in a peer marriage is that you can come to a peer decision about erotic inequality. Such inequality isn't coercion because it's taking place within the context of equality and collaborative decision-making. It's similar to a BDSM (bondage/discipline, dominance/submission, sadism/masochism) couple who practices consent, consciousness, and safety. A peer couple can re-narrate their sexual relationship to make it psychically unequal and therefore hotter. As true peers, they consciously embrace a different relationship in the bedroom.

Clients in both traditional and peer relationships who enter sex therapy are looking for a more satisfying sexual relationship. This often involves disrupting old sexual narratives that privilege the role of sexual desire and limit the integration of intimacy and sexuality.

As old narratives are challenged and transformed, possibilities open for couples to co-create new erotic experiences.

CHAPTER 2

⁂

EXPANDING THE HEALTHY SEX NARRATIVE

Our Internalized (and Unexamined) Model for Healthy Sexuality

The NRST approach examines how, as interpretive beings, individuals make meaning about themselves and others through the development of powerful personal sexual stories. Michael White (1995) emphasizes that, "it is the story or self-narrative that determines which aspects of our lived experience get expressed" (p. 13).

Our medical and psychological practices are responsible for promoting a major sexual health narrative, the Desire-Arousal-Orgasm Model, that imposes a rigid linear scheme on what's actually a complex multidimensional process. Most clients, heterosexual and LGBT, unknowingly internalize it as the only model of "healthy" sexuality. Inevitably, most people cannot sustain the linear sexual path this model requires, and many wind up in a sex therapy office feeling dysfunctional and broken. What clients (and some therapists) don't realize is that these clients are not broken, but the model they are using is not the right fit for them. Therapy needs to challenge the personal negative narratives this model creates and offer more expansive models that contain multiple pathways to erotic enjoyment.

Michael White's (1989) approach of *externalization of the problem* is essential toward this effort. He states:

> Externalizing, is an approach to therapy that encourages persons to objectify, and at times to personify, the problems that they experience as oppressive. In this process the problem becomes a separate entity and thus external to the person who was, or the relationship that was, ascribed the problem. Those problems that are considered to be inherent,

and those relatively fixed qualities that are attributed to persons and to relationships, are rendered less fixed and less restricting.

(p. 5)

One of the first questions I ask clients is:

"What sexual model are you using to determine what is healthy sex?"

This is how the externalization process begins. Just asking this question already signals to clients that there is more than one model (narrative) for healthy sexuality. An externalizing conversation that locates the "problem" outside the individual or couple, in this case the model of sexual health clients have internalized, begins to question the notion that something is inherently broken in themselves or the relationship. As clients attempt to answer this first question, I ask additional questions that disrupt the Desire-Arousal-Orgasm narrative, such as:

"Does desire have to happen for sex to start?"
"Does your body have to be aroused to continue sex?"
"Do you need to have an orgasm for sex to be successful?"

These questions are more rhetorical in that they begin to open a conversation about what sexuality is, where and when they learned the definition, how well it works for each partner, and who gets to decide what is healthy sex: Masters and Johnson? Helen Singer Kaplan? The DSM committee?

Most people are stumped by these questions. Why? Because most people aren't aware that they've internalized an idea of what sex should be like. They think sex is a universal natural act (Tiefer, 1995). Nowhere are models of sexuality more influential than in our belief about what constitutes a "healthy" sexual response. Most people are conditioned to believe that sex operates the same way for everyone and that it should unfold in certain predictable ways, but that's not the case. When I ask these questions, I'm both exposing and challenging the idea that there's one standard narrative about what is healthy sex.

When clients tell me they feel sexually dysfunctional, I'll say:

"I bet one of the reasons why you're sitting in front of me right now is that you're not experiencing desire, arousal, or an orgasm, right? I'll also bet that you're measuring your sexuality according to a model that was created by someone else. And your so-called dysfunction may be the result of trying to fit into a model that isn't working for you and that *shouldn't* work for you. The problem isn't you, but the model you've assumed is right."

It's crucial that therapists begin the process of transforming negative sexual narratives by first having clients examine their assumptions about sex.

Where It All Began: Masters and Johnson's Road to Orgasm

Whether we realize it or not, therapists have been profoundly influenced by the Masters and Johnson behavioral model that posits that everyone, regardless of gender, sexual orientation, gender identity, race, ethnicity, age, religious belief, or physical ability, basically acts the same way sexually. Relational sex therapists believe it is essential to expand the lens in understanding sexuality to include familial, social, historical, and intra-psychic influences as well.

In the 1950s and '60s, Masters and Johnson set out to document what constituted healthy sexual response. In a remarkable scientific feat at the time, they observed hours of laboratory-performed sexual activities by willing participants. The result of their effort was the development of the Human Sexual Response Cycle (HSRC), consisting of four phases of sexual response that they believed all men and women went through during sex (see Figure 2.1). For Masters and Johnson, sex starts with physical excitement. Nipples get hard, penises get hard, vulvas get wet. We plateau, then we have orgasm, followed by resolution.

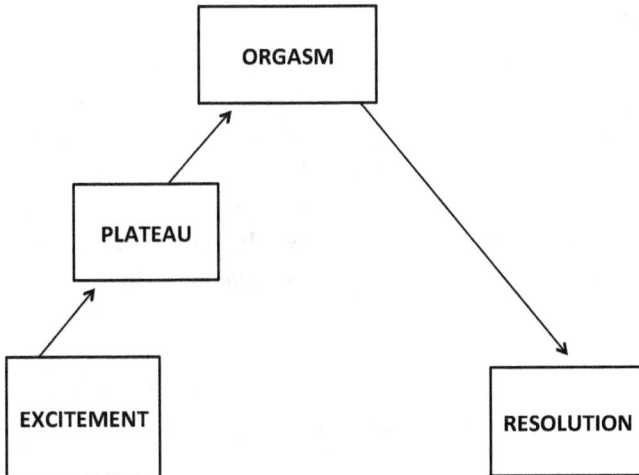

Figure 2.1

The HSRC focuses on orgasm as the goal of sex. Masters and Johnson believed that effective physical stimulation and removal of inhibitions was all that was required for successful sexual functioning. They helped develop sex therapy as a brief problem-focused therapy with sensate focus (progressive touching exercises) as its main technique.

Despite its popular appeal, the HSRC is quite limiting in its linear structure and its genital/orgasm focus. Many clients feel dysfunctional not because they really are, but because their sexual responses do not conform to the HSRC model. What if someone never experiences orgasm but feels very emotionally satisfied with sex? What if someone prefers non-genital over genital sexuality? What if someone never becomes fully aroused but feels connected with his/her/their partner? Are these experiences dysfunctional? Many people (and their partners) often think so.

The Masters and Johnson model creates problems for people – if they don't have an orgasm, they think something is wrong with either themselves or their partner. They may worry, "maybe my partner isn't really attracted to me or maybe my partner is having an affair."

What Masters and Johnson meant by excitement was physical excitement. Since they were a medical not a psychological team, the HSRC privileges and universalizes physical sexual response. Subsequent sexual models developed by psychologically trained professionals are more nuanced and multidimensional. There's a big difference between how a body reacts in a physical way and how it reacts when someone has a complicated sexual and emotional history, an unconscious, and particular attachment issues from childhood.

In short, the Masters and Johnson model imposes the "tyranny of the orgasm" (Loulan, 1984). Many clients I see in therapy have come to believe in the "Big O" as the only reason for having sex. This narrative can significantly impact a client's sexual self-esteem when they "fail." Preoccupation with attaining an orgasm often prevents a person from being fully present in the moment while having sex, which paradoxically often makes it more difficult to experience an orgasm. Instead of being in the moment, their mind says:

"Am I getting excited enough? I need to get excited more."
"Why isn't my partner getting excited? What am I doing wrong?"
"What if they don't have an orgasm, like last time? Is it me?"

The Masters and Johnson model is a linear one. We know from studying human development that sex cannot best be explained or understood in a linear way. A linear model assumes that a certain experience has to unfold in a sequential series of steps, which is not the case for most human experience.

Another limitation of the Masters and Johnson model is that it doesn't account for the particularities or contexts of an individual's situation in life. If an individual is taking an SSRI medication for depression, their experience of the HSRC may likely be altered. The same may hold true if someone is suffering the loss of a loved one, has a child who is challenged in some way, or is facing health or aging issues.

The Masters and Johnson model has also been criticized as unfriendly to women, but a lot of men I work with aren't helped by it either. Men who struggle with erectile functioning or ejaculation control, for example, often feel like performance failures. To help clients not feel broken, both men and women need more expansive models of sexuality and a narrative approach that presents sexuality in more expansive ways.

Helen Singer Kaplan: Putting Desire Front and Center

A subsequent sexual model, extending the HSRC, was proposed by Helen Singer Kaplan (1979), a psychoanalyst and sex therapist working in New York City in the 1960s and '70s. For Kaplan, sex didn't start with excitement but with something that happens *before* the body gets excited, called desire. Her work was so influential that desire disorders became part of our therapeutic language and were included in the *Diagnostic and Statistical Manual of Mental Disorders* (DSM). Kaplan developed a tri-phasic model that starts with desire, moves to physical arousal, and ends with orgasm (see Figure 2.2). Kaplan's model is still limited by its linear phase structure and orgasm endpoint, yet it helped therapists understand sexual functioning in a way that went beyond Masters and Johnson's physical model by introducing an internal, psychological component of sexual experience.

Since Kaplan's model was integrated into medical and psychological practice, many forms of desire disorders have been identified and treated by sex therapy. The number one problem I, and most sex therapists, see in our practices is not erectile dysfunction, premature ejaculation, or painful intercourse, but "desire disorders." Most common are discrepant desire cases, where one partner feels more desire than the other, or low desire cases, where neither partner feels desire, often leading to no-sex relationships. Many asexual clients have been pathologized when therapists misdiagnose them with hypoactive sexual desire disorder (HSDD) when their asexuality is a sexual orientation, not a disorder (Brotto & Yule, 2017).

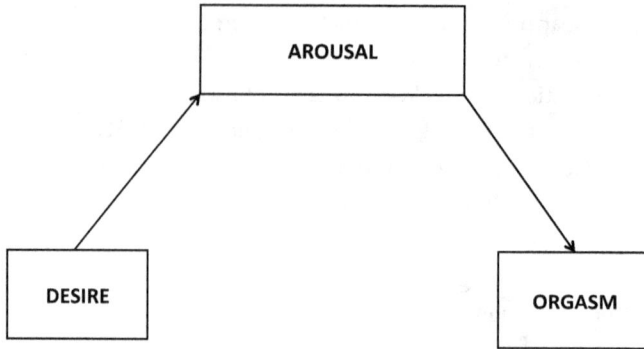

```
                    ┌──────────────────┐
                    │     AROUSAL      │
                    └──────────────────┘
          ┌──────────────┐        ┌──────────────┐
          │    DESIRE     │        │    ORGASM     │
          └──────────────┘        └──────────────┘
```

Figure 2.2

Despite the drawback of how privileging sexual desire helps create sexual dysfunction, Kaplan's contribution to the practice of sex therapy is monumental. Her seminal work expanded the practice of behavioral sex therapy to include psychodynamic and relational influences. Her case studies demonstrated the use of behavioral techniques like sensate focus, but in addition illustrated how to work with childhood and couple dynamics to enhance sexual functioning.

JoAnn Loulan's Sexual Model: Willingness and Pleasure

JoAnn Loulan (1984) was a Masters and Johnson trained sex therapist and couple therapist practicing in California who saw the HSRC model as a flawed one, especially for women who either weren't starting with desire as much as men were or experienced the goal of orgasm as problematic (or both). She worked mostly with bisexual and lesbian women; some of the bisexual women were in heterosexual relationships, so Loulan had experience with a wide range of sexuality. She felt there were too many "shoulds" in traditional sexual models that affected people's self-esteem and/or pressured them to conform. She wanted a model that gave people more options.

By starting with *willingness*, not desire, and ending with *pleasure* instead of orgasm (see Figure 2.3), Loulan's model expands sexuality beyond a physical response into an experience that focuses on one's subjective experience and agency in creating a fulfilling sexual experience. This model offers extremely powerful concepts.

In Loulan's model, one can *decide* to have sex and not wait until one feels "horny." This offers a revolutionary option for people, especially those who

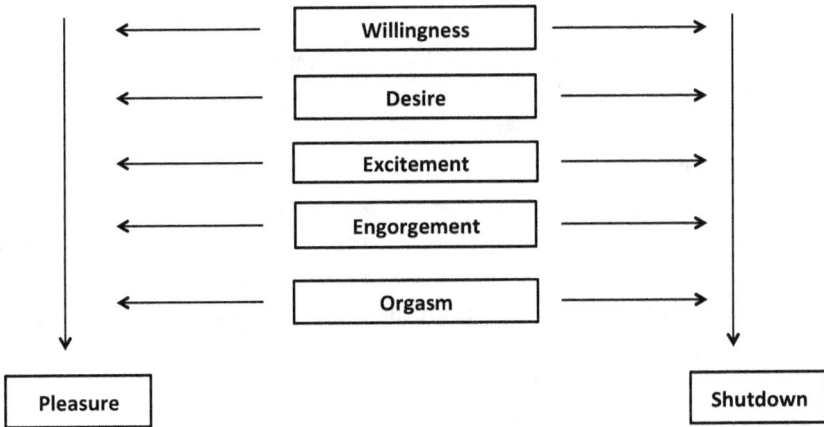

Figure 2.3

lose sexual desire over time in committed relationships. The *willingness* concept can give hope to survivors of sexual abuse who often find desire an
elusive, fraught experience. For survivors, willingness offers an option that
includes control, volition, and a way to communicate emotional and discur-
sive desire for their partners when the bodies cannot.

The *willingness* concept is also helpful when working with clients who
experience sexual aversion. In those cases the degree of willingness can be
measured on a continuum:

extreme aversion (–10) – neutral feelings (0) – enjoyment of sexual
initiation (+10)

The use of a *willingness continuum* normalizes a gradual process of development of willingness instead of the pressure of having to experience conflict-
free willingness right off the bat. That's too high an expectation for clients
(and their partners) struggling with sexual aversion.

Loulan's model normalizes shutdown at any point in the cycle and allows
movement back and forth between stages. It also replaces orgasm with pleasure as an endpoint that involves a subjective rather than physical experience.
Armed with this model, an individual can develop curiosity about one's
phases of sexual response in whatever order they emerge, whatever style of
initiating sex might be, and however one subjectively defines pleasure.

Loulan was not opposed to desire, but some people need to start with
willingness. Desire is a bodily sensation, a mysterious thing. Either you feel

it or you don't. Most people I see in my practice have never felt desire or haven't felt it for a very long time. And they don't believe they'll be able to feel it again. Having willingness as a normalized option to initiate sex gives the gift of sexual agency to clients. Once clients embrace willingness, I discuss initiation preferences and wishes to structure how sex will start. Some partners complain that they initiate sex to no avail; their partner says "no" and sex drops off the radar. In this case, I offer them the metaphor of sex as a game of tennis. If Partner A serves, Partner B can hit it back or not. If not, it's Partner B's turn to serve within the next seven days (the time can be altered depending on the sexual frequency pattern of the couple).

I'm somewhat of an outlier in the sex therapy field because I don't believe the goal of sex therapy should be to get desire back. It's another old narrative that we don't have to buy into. In fact, recent research has shown that desire isn't the first step for many women.

Instead, we can normalize willingness as a starting point for sex. Willingness is a cognitive function. In sex therapy we make the distinction between spontaneous desire and responsive desire. Spontaneous desire is the horny bodily feeling of really wanting sex. Responsive desire is when you feel desire in response to someone else's desire. If one partner feels desire, the other partner can say, "Sure, let's do it. You're feeling it and I'm not, but I know once I get started I'm going to enjoy it," sex will happen more often.

Research has shown that many women do not start with spontaneous desire. They start instead with responsive desire. For many women, desire *follows* arousal, it doesn't precede it (I will discuss this more when I discuss Rosemary Basson's model next). This makes willingness that much more important.

Partners can feel really badly about desire issues. Why doesn't my partner want me? Why don't I want them? With a more expansive view of sex, including narratives where desire isn't a given, you can get past that roadblock and have good sex. It's quite a relief for some to know that once partners start touching to arousal, desire may follow.

Loulan also makes an important distinction between sexual excitement and engorgement. Excitement is psychological, while engorgement is physical. It's important because there can be a great divide between psychological and physical arousal. Some people will become physically aroused – hard or wet, etc. – but their subjective psychological experience of arousal can be very low, only 1 on a scale of 10, for example. Their body is excited but they're not experiencing excitement. Or the other way around: they might subjectively feel very aroused, but that arousal may not be revealed physically by the body. This is called *arousal nonconcordance*. Chivers (2005) found that women experience nonconcordance to a greater extent than do men. It's not a dysfunction and shouldn't be pathologized. She also found that women get aroused by a greater variety of stimuli than do men.

As an example of how nonconcordance might look, a couple may come into therapy disagreeing about the sex they had. Partner 1 might say they had great sex and really enjoyed it. Partner 2 might say, "No, you didn't. You didn't enjoy it at all."

I'll ask Partner 2, "Why do you think your partner didn't enjoy it?"

"Well, they weren't physically aroused."

In this case Partner 1 felt quite aroused subjectively by everything that was going on. It was a psychological arousal, an emotional arousal, but it wasn't physical. That split is not unusual. It is important for therapists to educate clients about arousal nonconcordance. Someone who discusses sex research and makes arousal nonconcordance understandable in a fun, accessible way is Emily Nagoski (2015), in her book *Come As You Are*.

The endpoint in the Loulan model is pleasure, not orgasm. An orgasm is an objective physical experience. A muscle begins to pulsate and contract. Most people know when they're having an orgasm or not.

Pleasure, on the other hand, is not necessarily connected to a physical experience. It's a subjective experience. Clients often define it differently. For some people, pleasure is very "me based." In other words, what's happening in my body? For others, pleasure comes from feeling close to their partner or experiencing their partner's pleasure. Some clients report that experiencing their partner's pleasure is more important than having an orgasm. The pleasure resides in the emotional connection with the partner.

In a sexual model like Loulan's, there are no wrong or right definitions of sexuality or what makes a "good sexual experience." This allows for the exploration of more expansive narratives about oneself or a partner. It allows clients to change how they view sexuality, transforming narratives that prevent them from enjoying sex. Freed from the tyranny of the orgasm, clients are able to say, "Thank you, I've had enough for now," or "This feels fine." These statements communicate the sentiment of having had "good enough sex," a perspective advocated by sex therapists, Barry McCarthy and Michael Metz (2008).

Good sex means being able to be present, being able to communicate safely, and having fluidity about being in one's body and being with each other. Sex therapist Carol Ellison (2001) defines successful sex this way:

when the partners create erotic pleasure, to whatever level and in whatever form they desire on that particular occasion, and each ends up feeling good about him- or her-self and about the other; they both have a good time and enhance their relationship.

(p. 163)

Rosemary Basson: Arousal Before Desire

The latest conceptual revolution in understanding sexual response was developed by Rosemary Basson (2001). Her model emphasizes that male and female sexuality are different in terms of sexual motivation, sexual arousal, and sexual desire.

Unlike Loulan's model, which remains known mostly within feminist and sexual minority communities, Basson's female sexual response cycle has transformed mainstream sex therapy literature, challenging the traditional linear model of Desire-Arousal-Orgasm. Basson's circular sexual response cycle (see Figure 2.4) includes components such as multiple reasons for initiating or agreeing to sex, willingness to be responsive, psychological and biological influences on arousability, and the paradigm-shifting idea that *arousal may precede desire*. The research behind this idea was so convincing that hypoactive sexual desire disorder (HSDD) for females was dropped and replaced by female sexual interest/arousal disorder (FSIAD) in the DSM-5.

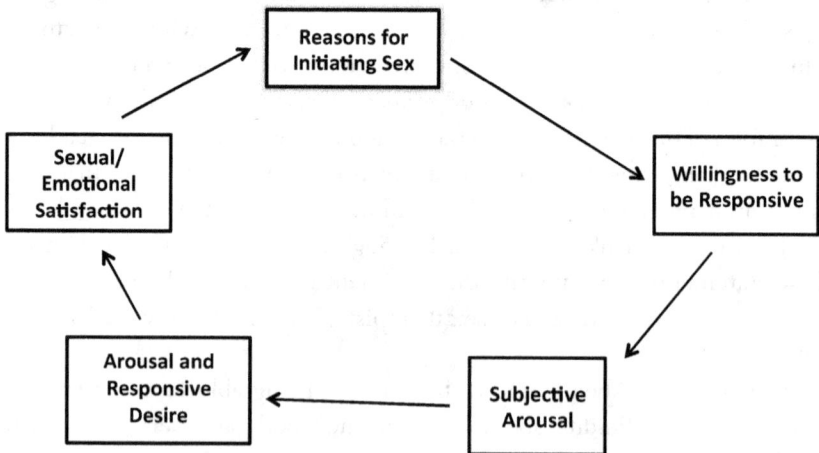

Figure 2.4

Basson's change in relationship between desire and arousal, differentiation between "spontaneous desire" (an innate drive) versus "responsive desire" (based on context and relationships), her recognition of the importance of subjective arousal versus physical arousal, and her endpoint of subjective sexual/emotional satisfaction are all contributions that give clients a greater range of sexual options to re-narrate a sexual life.

Even though both Loulan's and Basson's models were based on research on women, I offer both models as options for all clients (male, female, non-binary) who are struggling with negative sexual narratives associated with the Desire-Arousal-Orgasm linear sexual response model.

The Case of Nicole: Shifting Sexual Narratives for Transgender and Gender Non-conforming (TGNC) Clients

A male-to-female trans client, Nicole, was grateful to learn about willingness, pleasure, and connection as legitimate sexual components as she transitioned first with hormone treatment and then with Gender Affirming Surgery. Unlike arousal and orgasm, these subjective components can be unlinked from genital performance, a liberating expansion for some TGNC clients. These components and non-linear sexual response models gave Nicole a vocabulary to use with her partners and a normalizing set of sexual narratives as medical interventions sometimes altered her experience of her sexuality, genitals, and body. (See Erickson-Schroth [2014] for more about TGNC sexual relationship experiences.) At a recent conference on transgender experience and sexuality, Kate Bornstein and Barbara Carrellas (2019) stressed that "genitals do not define gender" (p. 8) and by extension they should not define sexuality, either.

Peggy Kleinplatz (2009), a Canadian researcher and sex therapist, has conducted some paradigm-expanding research on couples from a wide range of orientations and sexual practices who say they have optimal sexual lives. She identified eight major components of optimal sexuality from in-depth interviews. What's interesting is that none of the major components includes desire, arousal, or orgasm.

Instead, great sex included relational experiences like being present, being connected, communication, authenticity, vulnerability, and transcendence with their partner. It almost sounds spiritual – the feeling of being one and experiencing mutual and complete acceptance.

The main point is that clients need to be made aware of how they're behaving unconsciously according to some theoretical model or narrative (and not in some natural and universal way) and how this affects their sexuality. Do they consider orgasm as the only or best goal? Is genital sex the only "real thing"? Is all else a prelude to it? Is genital or anal sex incomplete without penetration? Is masturbation "sorry seconds"? By understanding their responses and those of their partner, they can be freed from judgment or pressure to measure up to the "right" sexual response.

Sometimes there will be difficulty in shifting from the desire/orgasm model to a willingness/pleasure/connection model. Some people may need to grieve that they may never feel desire, or that they may have to give up orgasms, or that they might not be able to be aroused as much as they would like because of a medical situation. Some people find it excruciating that their partner does not desire them. Some clients have told me that they don't want to have sex with their partners if they don't feel mutual desire.

Other people can more easily accept that their partner is shifting from desire to willingness. They're grateful that there's a model that gives them permission to be more expansive in their sexual lives. So many people come into sex therapy feeling there's only one healthy way to have sex. It's an amazing gift to be able to view sex in a much more open and ultimately fulfilling way.

CHAPTER 3

✳

THE SEXUAL HISTORY
Identifying Conscious and Unconscious Narratives

A person's conscious and unconscious sexual history plays out like a cacophony of voices every time they have solo or partnered sex. The sexual histories of partners are part of the chorus as well. Most people are not aware of these voices and the impact they have on sexual experience.

Sex is usually good at the start of a relationship, but as partners become more familiar with each other, sexual narratives unconsciously engage. Conflicts arise. Issues from the not-so-distant past are reawakened. Desire can diminish. As sex loses it novelty, conscious and unconscious stories come into play, and sex with a partner turns into group sex. Old narratives, thought to be buried a long time ago, re-emerge.

All sex is, in some form, an attempt to master childhood wounds (Stoller, 1985), a theme I'll return to throughout this book. People are all wounded in some way, and attempt to heal wounds, to various degrees, through sex. Clients are often unconscious of the fact that they're trying to work through some unresolved childhood drama through sexuality. They're unconscious both of the wounds they suffered and the ways in which they use, and sometimes misuse, sex in the struggle to heal them.

Everyone's history is interwoven into their sexual preferences. The person who likes to spank or be spanked is no more or less wounded from childhood than the person who likes only missionary sex. Missionary sex for some people may be used as a psychological defense, more so than the BDSM couple's sexual play. In the latter case, the couple may be mastering past wounds in a much healthier way.

Whatever people's histories might be, the drama of childhood wounds is played out in their heads in the bedroom:

"I never was sexy."
"My body is too fat."

"I don't like penetrative sex."
"We're a sexually dysfunctional couple."
"I'm simply not turned on by my partner."
"Sex makes me feel too vulnerable."
"My fantasies are perverted."

In this chapter I'll delve into the details of how therapists can help clients expose harmful sexual narratives that interfere with sexual fulfillment.

Although sexual narratives can seem daunting to address, therapists can do plenty of things in therapeutic work to help clients transform them. The heart of my approach is the relational sexual history. Without learning how to identify a client's conscious and unconscious sexual narratives, you can't help him/her/them become liberated from them. In this chapter I'll provide ideas and advice about how to process a client's traumatic memories and experiences, discuss the difference between privacy and secrecy, and describe ways to understand how someone's unique narratives have evolved from their past.

Uncovering the Client's Sexual History

I conduct an in-depth relational sexual history with every client who enters sex therapy at one time or another depending on the nature of the presenting problems clients bring into therapy. When working with couples I prefer to do so with each partner individually, not together. There are losses and gains conducting histories separately. One loses the empathy a partner might develop listening to challenges their partner faced in their life. However, much more importantly you gain the privacy most individuals need to be fully candid about their sexual life. There also are areas of sexuality considered to be healthy private parts like masturbation or personal sexual fantasies. In all, I'm trying to determine what each person's family of origin was like regarding bodily and emotional safety, emotional attunement, and attachment and how other relationships throughout life impacted on a person's sexual and relational narratives.

I start every sexual history with an essential question:

"What is your earliest memory of sexuality?"

I specifically use the term *sexuality*, not *sex*. If I ask for someone's earliest memory of sex, they will discuss behavioral examples – their first touch, their first kiss, maybe their first intercourse. When I say sexuality, I receive much more expansive responses. Some people will remember their first stirrings of attraction, their first wet dream, their first masturbation, or the first time they played doctor with a kid in the neighborhood. Maybe it was a memory of unwanted touch or viewing explicit sexual materials. Or maybe they overheard their parents doing something in the bedroom that sounded like daddy hurting mommy until they realized he wasn't.

People who had to deal with gender non-conforming childhoods will often tell me a gender story, not a sexuality story. People of color may start off with a racial development story or a story about skin color and attractiveness in their families.

Some people's memories go back to early grammar school or even earlier.

When a client offers their earliest memory, I slow things down to deeply explore the impact of that experience, probing the thoughts, emotions, and bodily sensations associated with it. Together, we examine the meaning the person made of the experience then, how the meaning developed into a narrative over time, and what they make of the narrative now.

As clients share their histories, I track certain themes. The first is boundary transgressions – experiences that made the individual feel out of control, scared, confused, disrespected, or hurt in relation to their sexual or self-integrity. Boundary transgressions can include physical, emotional, sexual, or verbal abuse, or more subtle derogatory messages about sexual orientation, gender non-conforming behavior, or associated with being male or female. The latter transgressions can include an off-hand remark by a parent, such as "Don't be a sissy" or "You look like a tramp in that dress."

I also track relational or attachment wounds. These emerge from experiences that left a person feeling betrayed, abandoned, neglected, or intruded upon emotionally, thereby impeding the development of safe attachment and intimacy.

The sexual history process usually takes two to five sessions. For many clients of all ages, the sexual history is the first time they thought about and shared their development as sexual beings with another person. Most couples never discuss their most private sexual stories.

Components of the Sexual History

Following are the major components of the sexual history, to be explored flexibly with the client in a fluid conversation, not by posing a list of questions.

Some of the components were adapted from *Sexual Dysfunction: A Guide for Assessment and Treatment* (Wincze & Carey, 1991).

Childhood: type of relations with family members; parental relationship; gender experience/identity/roles/expression; peer relations; first sexual feelings (same and/or other sex; trans or non-binary); masturbation; peer sexual play; sex education (how one learned about sex); religion/race/ethnic/class experience; messages about sex; how affection was shown; how nudity/body issues were handled; how privacy was managed; how boys and girls were treated; any unpleasant, confusing, embarrassing, or disturbing sexual/emotional experiences; medical treatments in self or family members; sexual/physical/verbal/emotional abuse or neglect; substance use.

Adolescence: peer relationships; school experience; experience of puberty; body development and image; menstruation; pregnancies or abortions; wet dreams; dating; self-esteem; masturbation (methods and fantasies); exposure to porn (including content); sexual behavior, attractions, identity (heterosexual, homosexual, bisexual, asexual, pansexual); gender expression/identity/role; coming-out experiences; first intercourse/sexual experiences; fantasies/dreams; how learned about sex; substance use.

Adulthood: medical history (including psychiatric treatment and psychotherapy); relationship history; sexual experiences; masturbation; porn use; fantasies; dreams; sexual problems (in self or partners); STIs; HIV status and safer sex; birth control; children (miscarriages, abortions, fertility issues); menopause; medications; substance use; occupational history; peer/family relations; coming-out experiences at home and work; online activity; kink preferences.

Societal Influences: the effects of biases based on race, ethnicity, sex, gender identity/role/expression, class, sexual orientation, religion, age, disabilities, and family form.

Current Sexual Functioning: current sexual functioning; areas of strength, difficulty, or concern, including any recent changes; sexual preferences; likes and dislikes about the partner and/or self; monogamy, polyamory; extra-marital sexual experiences; kink; non-sexual activities (individually and as a couple); communication about sex; intimacy and affection; love; sexual story about the present relationship; sexual goals for present relationship.

After getting the details of the client's first memory of sexuality, I ask about thoughts, feelings, and sensations at the time, if they were discovered or told anyone about the experience, and, if so, how the other person reacted. If not discovered, how might significant others have reacted?

Throughout the history I pay attention to themes of shame, guilt, and boundary violations, defined as anything that made the individual feel out of control, scared, disrespected, misused, blamed, or hurt in relation to their sexual/emotional/body/self-integrity.

A common reaction to an early trauma experience is self-blame, which is a way of having a sense of control over something for which the client wasn't responsible. It's a way of saying, "I couldn't stop my father/mother/ etc. from abusing me and I should have, so let me blame myself. At least I don't feel that the situation was completely out of my control, because that's too terrifying an idea." If the client identifies a particular experience that contains these themes, I then ask, "How do you think that experience affects your sexual/emotional life now? How has it influenced your feelings about yourself and/or your sexuality?" "Or, about your partner?"

I enter the sexual history process with an open mind, wondering:

- What is being communicated by this person through the maintenance of the couple's sexual problem?
- What childhood dynamics, including how the parents were as a couple, are influencing sexuality now?
- What sexual scripts and turn-ons developed in early life?
- How are attachment needs or fears being expressed or defended?
- Is the sexual problem an attempt at repairing a past wound or mastering some trauma?

These are some of the key questions I discuss with clients since they often serve as the foundation for re-authoring sexual narratives that contain shame, guilt, or self-criticism. I also utilize key psychoanalytic concepts, often explaining them to clients during history-taking to identify intra-psychic capacities or limitations that affect sex and sexual narratives.

Sexuality and the Flow of Connection and Separation

D.W. Winnicott (1971), the British psychoanalyst and object relations theorist, discussed the impact of "good enough" mothering. A child can experience secure separation and then come back and connect again with the safe base of the mother (caregiver). If a mother is well-enough connected to her child, the child can play securely in another room because the child knows that the mother is nearby and attuned to the child's well-being. Winnicott calls this "object constancy" because the child is securely internally connected with the mother. But if the child doesn't have that secure attachment with the mother, the child could experience trouble separating at all or with what we call rapprochement, which involves safely returning after separation from the mother.

There's a kind of sexual analogy to Winnicott's work about object constancy and connection that allows for psychic separation during sex. With really good sex a person can feel closely connected and attuned to a partner, like a child with a mother (I use the term "mother" to refer to a central caregiver of any gender identification/expression). At other times during good sex a person psychically "goes away" from a partner, focused on a part of the partner's body, or lost in a sensation, but doesn't feel insecure with that "separation."

However, if a person has difficulty with secure separation and/or reconnection, it can affect sexuality and even diminish desire. Desiring may be too risky when associated with attachment loss. If someone can't fluctuate between attachment and separation during sex, if they can't bear the loss of that safe space by losing themselves or the other in sex, then they may shut down sexually or avoid it entirely.

Does Secure Attachment Enhance Sexuality?

There's an ongoing debate in the sex therapy field about the association between attachment and sexuality. Some people make the argument that sex emerges from secure attachment (Gottman, 2015; Johnson, 2008). Couple therapist Sue Johnson would suggest that when a couple struggles with sexual disconnection, the therapist first works on creating a safe emotional bond between the partners. Sexuality emerges from creating that secure bond. Sue Johnson's work focuses on the need to co-create that safety in a partnership and how much sexuality depends on that co-creation.

Other psychotherapists argue that, paradoxically, a secure emotional bond can be a challenge to sexual passion (Mitchell, 2002; Perel, 2006). Psychoanalyst Steven Mitchell argued that our need for security and attachment can conflict with our need for sexual or romantic passion. It's not impossible for both to coexist, but in order for that to happen the tension between the two has to be consciously identified and processed by the couple. Without consciously engaging that tension, in Mitchell's view, a secure emotional attachment can threaten sexual passion, and vice versa.

As with most debates, the truth lies somewhere in the middle. Some clients require a level of security and safety in order to experience sexual passion, surrender, risk, or experimentation. Others compartmentalize their deepest passions and sexual abandon to experiences outside a secure relationship where there is little attachment or vulnerability and no possible negative relational consequences. Neither is inherently "healthy" or "unhealthy" and only needs to be understood and shifted if it causes distress to an individual or their partner.

Mirroring and Sexual Regulation

The Hungarian-born British psychoanalyst Peter Fonagy's (2008) major contribution to attachment theory is how secure attachment emerges from the parent-child mirroring relationship. In his article "A Genuinely Developmental Theory of Sexual Enjoyment and Its Implications for Psychoanalytic Technique," he notes how important it is for the caregiver to acknowledge and mirror the infant's emotional states. When this doesn't happen, the infant's emotional states remain potentially overwhelming.

> When mirroring fails because the caregiver's expression is inaccurate or unmarked or both, the infant internalizes a mismatched or amplified mental state as part of the self. These uncontained self-states create disorganization within the self and have to be projected out to be regulated.
>
> (p. 21)

The attuned parent helps the child learn about his/her/their emotional life and how to self-regulate one's emotional states, which is a very important skill to have.

Fonagy noted that parental failure to be attuned to their child's sexual development can have a profound impact on the child's sexuality. For example, a parent who is uncomfortable with sexuality may shame a child for masturbating or participating in some other sexual activity. If the parent doesn't know how to handle sexual behavior, the parent doesn't know how to mirror it and may wind up neglecting the child's sexual expressions. Most parents either don't know how or feel uncomfortable mirroring their child's sexuality, leaving him/her/them with a wrong message about sex. As a result, Fonagy argues that everyone is ultimately sexually dysregulated.

> Because emotional regulation arises out of the mirroring of affect by a primary caregiver and sexual feelings are unique in that they are systematically ignored and left unmirrored by caregivers, sexual feelings remain fundamentally dysregulated in all of us.
>
> (p. 11)

The point I emphasize with therapists is to be aware of sexual dysregulation not only in clients but also in oneself. It's important that therapists become aware of how they were or weren't mirrored sexually in childhood and what that means for countertransference when working with sexuality in psychotherapy. When a therapist makes errors in working with the sexuality of a client, it's usually because the therapist is sexually dysregulated in that moment. The therapist may feel threatened by the sexual material or aroused by it, and they don't know how to self-regulate at that moment because they didn't have that help from their parents when they were children. Given the paucity of sexuality content in professional psychotherapy training, teachers and supervisors in the mental health field, like neglectful parents, fail clinicians in how to self-regulate regarding sexual material. (In Chapter 9, I will talk about this issue in more detail and provide advice for therapists on how to maintain self-regulation and boundaries in psychotherapy.)

One of the functions of the therapist during sexual history-taking is striking a balance between curiosity, non-judgmental questioning, and identification of negative sexual narratives, functions that work best within a safe holding environment (Winnicott, 1971). Many clients report that one of the most profound experiences in the NRST process was narrating and understanding their sexual history with an interested, non-critical other, which is a first for most people. In many ways the therapist provides a corrective emotional experience by mirroring the client's sexuality in a way that they never experienced before.

Addressing Attachment Wounds in the Sexual History: "The Gleam in the Mother's Eye"

The sexual history often reveals that many clients didn't get enough love and attention as children. They may have had parents who were unhappy or even abusive. Other clients were lucky enough to get the nurturing and support they needed as children. Those people tend to be more resourceful, flexible, and resilient later on in life when sex and desire become more challenging.

Many children never received the "gleam in the mother's eye," a term employed by Austrian-American psychoanalyst Heinz Kohut in his 1966 article "Forms and Transformations of Narcissism":

> Before psychological separateness has been established, the baby experiences the mother's pleasure in his whole-body self, as part of his own psychological equipment.
>
> (p. 251)

Kohut went on to say that after psychological separation, "the child needs the gleam in the mother's eye" in order to pass successfully through succeeding maturation phases.

To me, Kohut is saying that a baby is affectionate and affection-seeking, and learns to be an independent "self-object" through being mirrored by the mother's (caregiver's) warmth of acceptance and closeness, often communicated not verbally but non-verbally through eye contact. Just by the way a caregiver looks at the child, they "hear" the message: "Bravo, you are here and you are worthwhile just as you are!"

When I use the phrase "the gleam in the mother's eye" during history-taking and later in couple sessions, clients often well up either with tears of recognition or with tears from deprivation. The well of emptiness clients live with when deprived of the childhood gleam in the eye is a crucial one to access and discuss as clients struggle with issues of feeling seen or unseen, accepted or unaccepted, desired or undesired by the (m)other in adulthood. It is sometimes heart-wrenching to observe how some clients cannot perceive a partner's "gleam" for them as they defend against a deep yearning for what they didn't get all those years ago. On some level they seem unwired to perceive the very thing they long for.

Another context where I mention the "gleam in the eye" is when couples become new parents. One configuration of the newly formed family triad is where one parent "falls in love" with the infant, offering that lucky child a consistent gleam in the eye as the infant develops. The other parent can often feel left out of the parent-infant love bond, feeling grief and/or anger at the loss of the gleam they had with the partner before the birth of the child. These feelings are often shared in private sexual history sessions since guilt may accompany feelings of neglect or deprivation by the partner. One client exclaimed, "I'm feeling competitive with my own child. How awful!" This provides an opportunity to normalize these feelings, to reduce the shame or guilt about them, and to explore how the client can discuss needs for emotional connection with their partner in a constructive way.

When back with the couple, I often initiate a general discussion about how to "share the gleam" between children and partners. Instead of only one parent offering the gleam to the child, the couple can learn how to become a "gleam team" as new parents. We also discuss how parents can learn to move between gleaming the child and gleaming each other. For many new parents nurturing the emotional and sexual gleam in their adult relationship while parenting small children is a major challenge. The sexual history material can be very helpful in identifying childhood narratives that limit such an integration of roles.

I work with many couples who approach sex therapy in a resilient way, moving back and forth between a willingness-based model and a desire-based model. They're able to initiate and enjoy sex either way. They have that flexibility from the beginning, once I explain it to them or give them support to use it.

Many other clients find the transition from desire to willingness a very difficult one. They are more inflexible in their relationship to desire, either in feeling it for someone or, more often, in experiencing their partner's desire for them. They don't feel desirable. And some clients can't embrace the willingness concept because it's too painful to accept (and not personalize) their partner's lack of desire for them.

When there's such a problem in flexibility, I return to the sexual history material. A problem with desire is often connected to not having had sufficient parental mirroring in childhood, the "gleam in the eye" that would have made them feel essentially desirable. Proper parental nurturing not only makes us feel loved but also desirable, not in a sexual way as children, but in a much larger way – as human beings. Children who are lucky enough to have a nurturing caregiver have an essential building block of self-esteem. They grow up feeling, "I'm a good person, I'm a valuable person, and I'm valuable not for what I do, but simply for who I am."

An adult who has this foundation will be more flexible in using a willingness model of sexuality. They will be less likely to feel threatened or challenged by it. It won't feel like they're being re-traumatized when they encounter a partner who loses desire. If a male partner doesn't have an erection, or can't have an orgasm, or never initiates sex, it can reawaken the parental rejection that his partner faced as a child. With a strong foundation in childhood nurturing, this is less likely to happen.

People may be unconscious about their sexual rigidity, and my goal in therapy is to make it conscious. They may tell me in the middle of a session, "I don't want to have sex without desire. I have to feel desire from my partner or it doesn't work." That's the most common example of inflexibility that I find. They'll take a very strident position, even if the other partner feels sexual attraction, wants to be sexual, is grateful for the willingness option, and is ready to practice it. Then I have to go back and do the work on the inflexible person's early years. The client often has to re-connect with the emotional devastation of the lack of the gleam in the caregiver's eye, grieve what they didn't get, feel the anger, and get the support, understanding, and patience from their partner to co-create the gleam in the present, a process that transforms the narrative that they are inherently undesirable.

People can become more flexible with age. When someone has had a narcissistic wound in childhood, the effects of that can sometimes be resolved or diminished over time. In addition, the narcissistic wounds associated with aging, bodies wearing out or breaking down, often has the effect of humbling people. The people I work with who are in their seventies and eighties are usually grateful to learn about the willingness model. They may not have felt desire for a long time because of surgery, chemotherapies, or antidepressants. They often are more flexible than younger people in embracing a non-genital, non-orgasm sexual menu.

Issues of Race, Class, Gender, and Religion

The sexual history exposes the complexity of each individual's sexuality.

It is important to understand the meaning of different sexual experiences within an individual's particular cultural background (Hall & Graham, 2013). Intersectionality comes to the fore – how interconnected and interdependent the social categories of race, class, religion, and gender are in creating systems of advantage and disadvantage. Sexuality and gender identity are situated within these social contexts, and it's important to listen for and help clients articulate how their experience of intersectionality developed.

One client I worked with was an Orthodox Jewish woman who felt conflicted between her religion and her bisexuality. She was married to a man while also exploring her emerging bisexual identity. She was in a terrible dilemma because both her religious community and bisexual community were important to her, but she felt embracing one meant losing the other.

This client's "resolution" resulted from finding an Orthodox group of gay/bi married women. When the 2001 documentary film *Trembling Before*

G_d premiered, about Orthodox Jewish gay people trying to reconcile their sexuality with their faith, she was afraid to go. What if someone saw her and outed her to her husband? But by this time she desperately needed the comfort of women who could understand her struggle. During the Q&A after the film, the client reached out to a female psychologist who spoke about a group she facilitated for gay/bi married Orthodox women. The client joined the group, and for the first time experienced a great depth of support and understanding – mirrored (to use an attachment term) for the first time for who she really was. Her depression and anxiety attacks lessened as she felt more integrated into the gay/bi Orthodox community.

In conducting the sexual history, I make sure to ask questions related to race and ethnicity. I advise you to have this same sensitivity. Ask clients directly: "How do you think your racial/ethnic identity relates to your sexual/gender identity and your sexual development?"

Some African-American clients talk about being aware of their own sexual attractiveness due to their skin color, which clashes with cultural or familial messages they received growing up. I've worked with male African-American clients who have had to deal with being stereotyped by the larger culture as hyper-sexual or sexual aggressors. How does that play out in a relationship if a partner wants them to be more aggressive? How do African-American women deal with the stereotype of being seen as loose or promiscuous?

As Herb Samuels, an African-American sex educator and professor at LaGuardia Community College in New York, pointed out during a May 2007 NPR interview:

> [T]here's always been a split within the black community about accepting your sexuality for what it is and in what it might be presented as to a larger community. . . . [I]t goes back to the [stereotype of the] hyper-sexuality of black men and black women in history. . . . [Y]ou walk a fine line where you want to have a satisfying sex life yourself but you don't want to be perceived as being overly due it. . . . [T]rying to come to grips with that and trying to develop a sexual identity that you're comfortable with oftentimes leaves [black] people in almost a sense of cognitive dissonance.
>
> (p. 5)

It's crucial to explore with clients if/how race contributes to this dissonance.

Class also should not be left out of sexual history questions. Some working-class women in therapy describe how their sexuality was influenced by very strict gender roles that they ascribe to their class background. One woman explained, "In my childhood, men were men and women were women, and if the woman was unhappy in their marital relationships, too bad. A man could look for sex outside the marriage, but the woman could not." The husband in this case ran the show due to a class-based value system. Middle- or upper-class women often have a lot more autonomy, power, and resources when they're dissatisfied with sex, although that doesn't necessarily translate into an entitled sexual agency. Sometimes gender roles override class advantages. It's crucial to explore these issues as they manifest uniquely for each client.

The Case of Anne and the Impact of Attachment Wounds

The main goal of the sexual history is to identify attachment wounds that affect sexual relations in adulthood. One lesbian woman told me her earliest memory of sexuality was when her beloved Nonno (maternal grandfather) was dying when she was twelve years old. As Anne told me her story, I wasn't sure at first how it related to sexuality.

"At the time he was dying," she told me, "my sister got pregnant out of wedlock."

She grew up in a very devout Italian Catholic family where there was a lot of shame about the pregnancy. Everything became focused on how to handle the pregnancy. Anne received scant attention or comfort from her mother while her Nonno was dying in the other room.

There are stories in our lives and there are narratives. The story is what happened. The narrative is one level up: what did the story mean to us? How did we interpret it and how did that interpretation affect us? Anne was clear on the meaning of her story.

"I knew I was in big trouble sexually in the family," she told me. "If my parents were so ashamed of my sister's pregnancy that they neglected Nonno as he died, how would they react to me liking girls? There was no use in revealing who I was."

As an adult, Anne was able to look back at her narrative and understand how it organized her life: as a child in a family that was preoccupied with sexual shame and traditional values, she wasn't going to make it as a girl who was into girls. She began drinking and taking drugs in adolescence, and wound up hospitalized at one point. Anne's parents didn't have a clue about what she was dealing with. And Anne didn't fully realize it either until she examined the memory of her Nonno's death in therapy with me. It took her a while to unpack that memory and its associated narratives about the unacceptability of her lesbianism and how it's best not to express one's true self.

As mentioned before, I spend quite a lot of time on the first memory. I try to get a sense of what it was like for the client as a child. If you played doctor, how did it feel? Did you enjoy it or not? Was there any shame? Guilt? What kind of story were you telling yourself then? What were you sensing in your body? Did a parent or sibling walk in? Did they say anything? If they didn't say anything, what was their expression or mood? Our narratives can be powerfully formed not only by what a significant other says or does, but by what they didn't say or do. Silence around sexuality can cause a great deal of guilt and shame.

I ask about three levels of experience – thinking, feeling, and sensing – when clients share sexual stories from the past. These levels are also an important part of the mindful touching process I'll explain in Chapter 5.

Through the sexual history, I'm constantly tracking major patterns and themes. How did the client feel about their body as a child? Was their emotional safety compromised? Was sexual safety challenged? Was there any physical abuse?

From the earliest memory of sexuality, I begin to get a sense of how the child developed, not only in terms of sexuality but also how they felt as a little being in the world.

The Case of Jason and the Impact of Religious Sexual Shame

Jason came to me with serious erectile problems. His first memory of masturbation was not a positive one. His father, a minister in an esteemed local church, caught him masturbating, dragged him out of the bedroom, and sat him in the living room with the Bible. "That's a sin and don't you ever do it again," his father told him. "You read the Bible and don't move until I tell you." Jason was further humiliated because his mother and siblings witnessed the scene.

When his girlfriend touched his penis, Jason couldn't get hard. His bodily narrative didn't associate the penis with pleasure, only with sin and shame. He had lived with this bodily narrative his whole life without realizing it.

Many clients, like Jason, carry unknown narratives that are deep-seated. That's why the sexual history is so important to begin a process of discovery and disclosure.

Externalizing the Problem During the Sexual History

The goal of NRST is to shift clients' narratives about their sexuality so they can re-author their lives. I start this process by externalizing a problem first during sexual history-taking and then in couple sessions.

In this process, the problem becomes objectified; it can be viewed as a separate entity external to the person or relationship that's experiencing the problem. Through externalization, people no longer view their problems as fixed and inherent to who they are (or who they think they are). When the problem is externalized, they become less negatively fixed in their views about themselves, helping them more easily make changes that they desire.

An example of using externalization would be with a gay couple having conflict involving low sexual desire. What they might not realize is that underneath their conflict is unacknowledged shame and trauma from their coming-out experiences in their families. They both got the message that there was something wrong with gay sex. They entered into their relationship with an unconscious sense of shame that translated into sexual avoidance.

The problem could seem to be with the couple, when it's actually rooted in homophobia they experienced as young gay boys. The real problem is the damage done by societal and familial homophobia, not with each partner's sexuality or with the relationship. When the problem is externalized and attributed to homophobia, the partners may begin to shift their belief, about "being broken" and can become allies in rooting out their internalized homophobia.

Whether therapists use the term externalizing or objectifying, they're basically doing the same thing – taking the problem outside the individual or couple. The couple is then able to bond as allies and work together as a team against the externalized problem because it has been depersonalized, making it easier to discuss and address. Unproductive conflict often decreases, difficulties become lighter and less serious, and people have greater confidence that they can solve their sexual problems.

Privacy Versus Secrecy

Before I start individual sexual histories I discuss with clients the possible number of individual sessions we may need. I also ask them how they will feel if some of the information discussed in the separate sessions remains private. Some clients express very strong opinions about privacy versus secrecy that were never discovered until now.

I take time having partners discuss how they define both, just as I have them discuss their definitions of monogamy. In the age of the internet, sexting, and widespread pornography, these are important discussions to have. Many couples neglect to talk about privacy, secrecy, and monogamy, let alone define them.

Those kinds of discussions usually take place after a crisis — one partner finds porn or evidence of an affair on their partner's computer. Someone may feel they're being monogamous as long as they don't have physical contact with someone outside the relationship. For other people, the definition is stricter or looser.

When I conduct a sexual history with a partner individually, we explore private areas. Some private areas of inquiry that are important for me to explore (i.e., sexual fantasies, masturbation history, past peak sexual experiences) don't need to be disclosed to a partner. Information that is secret (something going on that negatively affects the relationship), if shared with me, would be discussed to understand what it means, how it affects the couple's relationship, and if/how to proceed with couple sex therapy.

Some people can tolerate the idea that their partner might have a private sexual life or private sexual thoughts and fantasies. Others are troubled by the thought. One client told me, "My partner shouldn't fantasize about anyone but me," or another said, "Why masturbate when you're in a relationship? That's a betrayal."

I resist taking the position that there's a right or wrong perspective regarding these questions, even though some clients attempt to recruit my support. Rather, my goal is to help people talk about their feelings and work out their differences. My job is to listen to it all and help clients clarify the reasons they have certain positions. Some positions are often developed from experiences in childhood, sometimes involving issues in the parental couple.

There can be strong differences of opinion about pornography. For some people it's a real crisis if they find their partner using it. For others, it's not a big deal. In the sex therapy field, we sometimes suggest that people use erotica or porn to expand their sexual menus or increase arousal. It's not often viewed as a harmful thing to do or as a betrayal of the couple relationship. However, it is important to understand the histories and values of clients before suggesting such a therapeutic option.

For other people, pornography raises deep moral issues. If one partner thinks it's immoral, my role is to help that couple deal with that difference, in the same way they might have to discuss differences about how to spend money or raise the kids.

Some people don't want their partners to know when they masturbate, how often, and what they're thinking about, even if they've been together for many years. They feel they're entitled to their private sexuality and there's nothing wrong with that. That's not a secret per se, although if masturbation is negatively affecting partner sex it is important to pursue as a couple issue.

The difference between privacy and secrecy is that the latter affects the relationship. A present affair would be one example. Or if a husband tells his wife he's staying up late to do some work but is instead indulging his porn habit. If he prefers porn to couple sex, then that's a secret that the couple is going to have to confront and work on.

Viagra use can be a point of contention. If a man is ashamed about having erectile issues and takes Viagra secretly, some partners feel that's a breach of trust and openness. Other partners aren't bothered by it.

Before I work on the sexual history with each partner, I talk to the couple about what we're going to do with the sexual history information. I tell each partner, "You can share information with me and some of it can be private, or you can share information with me and it can all be transparent." This opens a compelling conversation if partners differ on what they would like. As a therapist, I have to be clear with the couple so I don't wind up being held hostage holding information that is affecting the couple process. (For more information on secrets in psychotherapy, see Imber-Black [1998]; Scheinkman [2005].)

In over thirty years of practice, affairs have been an infrequent secret. Most people who want an affair to remain secret either don't enter sex therapy or don't tell the therapist. If they do tell me, I understand it as a way of asking for help in either ending the affair or addressing it and the issues surrounding it in the couple.

Secrets more often are usually tender and intimate things that people have trouble sharing with their partners, such as:

"His penis is too small and I can't feel it. I've never gotten any pleasure from him inside me. How could I tell him that? It would destroy him."
Or, "I hate the way she kisses, but I can't bear to tell her."
Or, "I'm still so attached to my ex that every time I'm making love with my partner, I think of them. If my ex showed up single right now, I might even consider leaving my partner."

These kinds of issues can be very challenging. People often feel heavy-hearted revealing them; they believe there's no way out. I work on developing a sense of balance. How can we shift such an issue from the foreground into the background and proceed with developing the sexual connection in the couple?

Sometimes this means that one of the partners needs to do individual work with another therapist. Sometimes I'll see a person individually after I complete the sexual histories, if it's agreed upon with the partner, to work on a limited specific issue that is affecting the couple's progress. For example, some people who have a lot of sexual anxiety can be helped by doing mindfulness work with me alone. The partner doesn't have to be present.

Other people suffer from terrible guilt and shame about certain sexual fantasies. They've never told anyone about them, and they believe that these fantasies are sick and perverted. I might spend some time with this person individually to explore how to transform their narratives about the fantasies that negatively impact couple sexuality.

Dealing With Trauma Issues

Sometimes I'll find out something about one partner – something private, not necessarily a secret – that's affecting their sexual functioning. A history of trauma is a good example. Some people never told their partners because it was too difficult to reveal.

It's important to work on trauma issues to create safety, so that the other partner knows what a flashback is and how to provide support if and when it happens. Sometimes I recommend the survivor receive some individual trauma therapy with another therapist before we delve into sex therapy. If sexual desire is affected by trauma, willingness will only work when someone has a sense of safety.

I may learn about trauma in an initial couple session or during an individual sexual history session. It could be physical abuse, sexual abuse, or rape; it could be sexual or non-sexual trauma. It could be early in life or later in life. Trauma could be one incident or many incidents over a period of many years. The important point is how the individual experienced the trauma, what narratives they created as a result, and how they affect their sexuality and intimacy now.

Once trauma is disclosed, I explore the client's therapeutic history in relation to the trauma. Have they had individual therapy? Trauma therapy? Support group experience? Eye Movement Densensitization and Reprocessing (EMDR) or Somatic Experiencing (SE) therapy?

I'll continue my assessment by asking how the trauma affects them. I ask questions such as:

"How much does your partner know?"
"How has the trauma affected your sex life? Emotional life?"
"Do you know what triggers you?"
"What are your major triggers? Visual? Auditory? Smell? Taste? Part of the body? A particular sexual context or sexual position?"
"Do you know what dissociation is?"
"Do you know what a flashback is?"
"If you have a flashback, what do you need to recover?"
"Do you have flashbacks with a partner or when masturbating or both?"

I thoroughly unpack these issues because the more a person can articulate these concepts and have a sense of their needs, the more they'll feel safe proceeding with sex therapy. A person having a flashback may not want to be touched or even spoken to. The partner might be most supportive by leaving them alone: "I love you, honey. I'm in the other room if you need me." Some people need to be alone; other people need to be held. Needs and responses vary greatly.

As I'm compiling histories and identifying narratives, "then and now questions" open up our discussion: "How did you feel about that childhood incident at the time? How do you think it's affecting you now?" Some people don't know and others are convinced the trauma and its effects are in the past.

They may have been in a relationship for many years and have never told their partners about the trauma. They feel ashamed. It's too upsetting to reveal. It can take time to establish a sense of safety in order to bring that material into the couple's work.

I worked with a lesbian named Mary who had been sexually abused in her childhood. She didn't want to share that history with her partner. "I've already worked on that in therapy," Mary said to me. "My partner knows a little bit about it but not much, and it's not affecting my sexuality."

I said, "Okay, how about we make a deal? We'll go into the work without you talking about it. If you're not reaching the results you want in six months or a year from now, you'll tell me. Then we can meet individually and talk about the abuse and its possible effect on the relationship to see if you're willing to bring it into the couple work."

It can be challenging to develop a sexual menu with a trauma survivor, and especially in a couple containing two trauma survivors. They are dealing with two sets of triggers at any given moment, two kinds of dissociation, two kinds of flashbacks, and sometimes two different sets of needs for recovery.

This requires special care in co-creating a sexual menu. I often first ask trauma survivors to individually construct a menu that articulates items that help him/her/them feel emotionally and sexually safe. This provides the foundation for a mutual menu that provides safety for both partners. (I discuss creating a sexual menu with trauma survivors in more detail in the next chapter.)

Identifying Intergenerational Trauma

The sexual history sometimes reveals *intergenerational transmission of trauma*. To name a few examples, I would inquire about the following: Jewish clients and their historical relationship to the Holocaust, African-Americans and their relationship to slavery, first and second-generation immigrants and their family stories about the process, and Japanese-Americans and their relationship to World War II and U.S. internment camps. Trauma from past generations may manifest in the present as depression, anxiety, anger, or safety issues, all of which may impact sexuality.

Someone's family history may include a relative who was raped or abused, or who experienced tragic illness or death. A person in the next generation could be carrying that history and living out the sequelae in the present relationship.

The genogram is a helpful tool to identify family themes across generations. For example, if I'm working with LGBTQ adolescents or young adults who are struggling with coming out, understanding their family system could help them identify the right persons to tell at first. Maybe it's not mom or dad but an aunt or uncle who is particularly open-minded, or who broke with family expectations in a different way.

Reviewing the Sexual History

Conducting the sexual history usually takes four or five sessions. Sometimes a person is not yet willing to share something but may be able to do so in the future, when they're more grounded in the couples work. Building trust for full disclosure often takes some time. When the individual history is completed, I review it with the client alone:

"What narratives have we discovered?"
"What narratives should we share with your partner which most likely are affecting your sexual life?"
"What information would you like to keep private for now?"

I make it clear that they have control over what gets shared. It is, after all, their sexual story to tell. I will have an opinion about what should be shared but not a final vote. I don't share anything without permission, which is crucial for establishing trust. As I stated earlier, if the client reveals a secret that impacts the couple, we will discuss how that affects the plans for couple sex therapy.

Sometimes people don't have an answer to how certain narratives affect their sexual life now. They may say, "I have no clue." And I'll respond, "That's okay, just leave that question in your mind." Several months later they may discover a profound connection about their narrative and how it's affecting them sexually. That's the power of exploring one's sexual history.

In the narrative integration sessions that follow, each partner shares, with my help, the stories and narratives that are central to their current sexual difficulties. It is an opportunity for partners to disclose particularly intimate stories within a safe relational environment. For many people this is the first time they are hearing an abuse story or shaming experience of their partner's and they welcome the opportunity to express empathy for their partner's wounds. Even though there still can be anger or hurt in how their partner has made them feel undesirable, rejected, or pressured sexually, it often helps for people to understand how many of the narratives shaping the destructive patterns in the relationship were created from experiences long before they met. With empathy and compassion, defenses soften, and partners realize how they co-created and/or co-maintained their sexual problems. After this process, they are often ready to begin treatment as allies in their erotic journey.

CHAPTER 4

❋

DECONSTRUCTING SEX WITH THE
SEXUAL MENU

After the sexual history, the next important tool I use to help people change false and damaging sexual narratives is the sexual menu. It enables clients to become aware of their sexuality, their preferences, and what they wish to experience with their partners. It helps partners communicate honestly and openly about their sexual needs and desires.

Many couples don't communicate about their sexual preferences and wishes. I've worked with couples who have been together ten, fifteen, and twenty years and who never have had one intimate conversation. They don't know what their partner really likes. They don't know if their partner is enjoying sex. They're timid about bringing up their wishes and desires, whether it's trying a new position or anal sex. Without good communication about sex, it's easy for misunderstandings to fester.

The sexual menu gives couples the opportunity to safely talk about their sexual wishes, hopes, excitements, and concerns in a creative and playful way. Together with the concept of "willingness," the sexual menu can help dormant sexual lives become re-connected. What are two people willing to try, do, give, receive, or share? What are they willing to discover together as non-judgmental experimenters? How can you, their therapist, guide them as curious explorers in the realm of the erotic?

Clients tailor the sexual menu to their needs, as a couple and as an individual. There are many kinds of menus — safety menus, trust menus, intimacy menus, vulnerability menus, playfulness menus, and more. If a client is struggling with erectile difficulties, I'd ask him to first construct a sexual menu whose items do not depend on a hard penis. Or, if a woman reports trouble with painful vaginal intercourse, I'd suggest she construct a vaginal penetration-free sexual menu. This permits people to be able to start partnered sexual contact without concern about the difficult body part that in the past often ruined all sexual activity.

The first thing the sexual menu assignment does is help the client think about him/her/themself as a sexual being. I ask each partner to sit down at home with a pad and a pencil and, in a very broad and open way, write down whatever they associate with the words sexual, sensual, and erotic. I urge them not to worry about what they write, whether it might be "too vanilla" or "too kinky." I tell them to forget what I might think (I've heard it all) or how their partner might react (they won't be permitted to at first). I say, "Think of your five senses. Think of what you might enjoy looking at, listening to, tasting, smelling, and touching. List as many items that come to mind."

The menu can include bodily sexual acts, such as intercourse, but it can also include things that aren't bodily based, such as looking at a sunset together. For some people, cooking food and eating it together makes them feel sensual, erotic, and connected.

Clients may not know initially how to define the words *sexual*, *sensual*, and *erotic*, but by free-associating they end up compiling a list that captures what those words mean to them. It doesn't matter whether the list is long or short. There's no right or wrong way to do this exercise. The important thing is that the client lets him/her/themself go and writes down whatever comes to mind.

I ask each partner not to share their lists with each other after they complete them individually. At our next appointment I ask one partner to read his/her/their list and discuss it with me, while the other partner listens without speaking or commenting. It usually takes an entire one-hour session to review one person's menu, even if it's a short one. I ask questions about the items along the way. For instance, if a client reads "kissing" as an item, I might say, "kissing can include light kisses, deep kisses, with a tongue one way or the other, or both. What do you like?" I ask this question and ask for more detail to encourage clients to elaborate about how they like a particular item done.

I'm not only discussing the partner's menu items, but also role-modeling for both partners how to have a curious and non-judgmental conversation about sexuality. Not many couples are able to have that kind of conversation. When the session is over, I ask them not to talk about the session or their menus at home. Initially, I want this to be an individual process, without influence from the other partner. In the next session, the second partner reads and discusses his/her/their menu while the first partner just listens.

In the third session both partners share questions and feelings about the menus. Were they surprised? Confused? Delighted? I pay attention to how partners communicate. If judgment surfaces either toward themselves or the other, I gently intervene to suggest a way to say something that is more a question than a comment, more curious than critical. If the judgment continues, I encourage the person to share more about deeper concerns or fears that may underlie the judgment.

It's very important to do the sexual menus after the sexual histories because having background material helps you to navigate issues as they arise. For example, if I know from the history that one partner has an issue with oral sex and can't talk about it with their partner, I'm prepared to delve into oral sex as a menu item whether the client brings it up or I do.

For example, let's say a woman likes to give oral sex but not receive it. She can't talk to her husband because he's deeply upset about it. If the woman has oral sex on her menu, I can say, "Oh, let's hold it right there. With oral sex, some people prefer to give, some prefer to receive, and some like reciprocal oral sex. There's nothing right or wrong with any of those preferences. How about you?" The woman might say, "Actually, I'm fine giving but not really receiving." Now the ice is broken and we can process that in couple sessions in the future. If that same woman doesn't list oral sex at all, after she reads her list I might say, "I noticed your list doesn't include oral sex. Let's discuss what preferences or not you have about it."

Through this type of discussion I'm modeling for them the process of talking about sex. Perhaps for the first time they're really hearing from each other and learning from each other about their sexual likes and dislikes in a non-judgmental way.

I worked with a couple who had been married for ten years and hadn't had oral sex since very early in their marriage. The husband had given his wife oral sex in the beginning and she seemed not to like it; they never talked about it and he never gave her oral sex again. He was shocked to find out from her sexual menu that she liked receiving oral sex. In the discussion afterward, he said he was surprised to hear she liked it. She asked him why he thought she didn't, and he said she didn't move or say anything to indicate she was enjoying it. This gave her a chance to educate him about how silence during sex often meant she's in a deep state of pleasure. Again, the sexual history provided valuable information for the sexual menu exercise. Knowing her history of deep silent pleasure and his insecurity about her silences, I was prepared to help them expand the conversation with a non-critical open spirit.

Many people don't talk about their sex lives together because they worry about seeming to reject their partners or being rejected, or because they think something's wrong with their sexuality. For example, some hetero-sexual men won't talk with a partner about their desire for receptive anal sexuality because they feel that it's a gay thing.

This situation presents an opportunity for me to do a little sex education. First, I'd inform him that sexual orientations do not line up with specific sexual activities. A heterosexual man who enjoys anal sex is not "secretly gay." Second, I'd tell a man who has concerns about discussing his desire for receptive anal sex that he doesn't have to bring it up in our sessions; I can bring the issue up for him during the sexual menu exercise by saying, "How is anal sexuality for the both of you? Some people like it, giving or receiving or both. How about you?"

Another way to use the sexual menu is to encourage clients to explore pleasure without penetrative sex just to expand their sexual options beyond penetrative genital sex. People who have had post-cancer treatments and medications, or experienced sexual trauma, can lose their ability to enjoy penetrative sex. When partners are truly relaxed, present, and excited with-out the pressure to genitally perform, there are many ways to sexually con-nect and experience pleasure, and the sexual menu can help them in this discovery. When discussing the centrality of intercourse, I often mention the book *Let Me Count the Ways* by Klein and Robbins (1999) that celebrates "outercourse," the pleasures of non-penetrative sex, including sensuality and intimacy through touch.

After discussing each partner's individual list, the next assignment is to make a combined sexual menu for the couple from their individual menus. Whatever doesn't end up on that list because one partner doesn't want it at the moment can be discussed at a later point. My goal is to have them come up with a list that they both can put into practice immediately, whether it's kissing and hugging, a walk on the beach, or a non-genital massage. If they want to become more physical, they can with the first round of the couple sexual menu.

Some people, even if they've made a list together, feel much safer if I assign them a menu item to explore and suggest a time limit as a container for the experience. I usually start with five-minute experiences and expand as clients seem ready. There is no rush. The goal is for clients to become more comfortable with a variety of menu items while developing trust in each other as an erotic team.

Other clients are more spontaneous and playful about it from the start. They'll write their menu items on slips of paper, put them in a hat, and pick one. Sometimes the choices need preparation. One woman wanted her partner to dress up like a fireman and he needed a few days to get the equipment.

What's most powerful about the sexual menu is that it changes the way couples view sex.

It deconstructs sex (as something only genital, penetrative, orgasmic) and expands it to include a broad array of physical and non-physical intimacies. It enables them to directly communicate their desires and hesitations without fear of judgment or shame. If a man is having ejaculation concerns ("too short" or "too long"), for example, I'll suggest he initially list non-orgasmic items. If a woman experiences painful intercourse, she can select items that she finds sensual and erotic that don't include penetration. While the woman is working on exploring how she could have non-painful penetration, she and her partner can still start becoming an erotic couple again. The same thing with a man who has premature ejaculation or erectile difficulty; while dealing separately with those issues, he can still please his partner. No longer is the couple's sex life held hostage by their areas of difficulty. We're not giving up on solving problems; rather, we're merely removing the pressure to perform in ways that aren't comfortable or that shut people down. We're merely starting with the path of least resistance.

With the sexual menu, sex becomes playful and relaxed, rather than something that's shameful, fraught, or avoided and never discussed.

Using the Sexual Menu With Kris and Justin

Of course, there's a catch: most couples feel deeply uncomfortable at the prospect of sharing their sexual preferences with each other. Many have never even thought about their erotic preferences, much less felt safe enough to express them openly. Typically, my clients respond with some version of: "You want us to do what?!"

That was the reaction of Kris and Justin, the couple I introduced you to in Chapter 1, who started out really hot but who hadn't had sex in over a year when they came to see me. "This is way too private," was Kris's first response to the sexual menu.

I explained that the sexual menu would help them learn to communicate more freely about their erotic preferences and be more flexible about sexual choices. When they still looked uneasy, I pulled out my most persuasive metaphor – comparing sex to food.

"Imagine going to a restaurant and ordering the same thing from the menu each time," I said. "You're likely to get bored. If your partner prefers Chinese food and you prefer Italian, you don't make one feel superior to the other. You take turns going to each restaurant. Sometimes, one partner may want a full meal and the other just wants a few appetizers. That's usually okay. And sometimes one person isn't very hungry but accompanies their partner to the restaurant to keep him or her company."

Now that they were both smiling, I told them to go home and individually write a list of all of the activities they could think of that they found sensual or erotic.

"No holds barred," I told them. "No worries that an activity may be too kinky or too tame. There are no 'right' or 'wrong' menu items."

I encouraged them to think beyond genital involvement and to list activities that stimulated all the senses: visual, tactile, auditory, olfactory, and gustatory. My final instruction: "Don't share your lists at home. We'll do it together in session."

When Kris and Justin arrived at our next session with no menus in hand, I surprised them by saying that it didn't matter. "Your trouble with the exercise is very useful," I told them. "It's a win-win. If you complete the menus, you move closer to a sexual connection. But if you don't, you learn what keeps you from connecting sexually. That's important information."

When I asked why they thought they hadn't finished, both described situations in which they felt sexually rejected and hurt by the other. "The truth is," Kris said, "I'm scared to tell Justin what I want because I'm afraid he'll criticize me." After a brief silence, Justin said, "Me too." The genuine apologies they exchanged at the end of the session allowed them to move forward.

When the couple brought in completed menus a week later, I congratulated them and explained that each partner would read his or her list aloud while I asked some clarifying questions. The other partner would remain quiet and simply listen. "Doing it this way allows each of you to have the floor without being interrupted or trying to deal with your partner's reactions," I said. The approach also allows the listener to observe the therapist conducting a non-judgmental conversation about sexuality with his or her partner. I've found that almost without exception, the listener pays close attention to this exchange.

Kris was too self-critical to allow Justin to give her oral sex, so she avoided it completely. Justin assumed she didn't like oral sex so he never pushed the topic, although he felt rejected and disappointed. When Kris read out "oral sex" from her menu, I asked if she'd be willing to stop there so we could talk a bit about it. When she nodded, I said, "You know, some people like reciprocal oral sex, while others prefer to only give or receive." In response, Kris began to talk about her deep fear of receiving. Eventually, she said, "I think it's connected to my mom's hypercritical comments about my body." Turning to Justin, she said, "I'd actually love to give you oral sex if you can accept it one way – at least for now." Justin grinned in surprise and delight. He assured her that he would put no pressure on her to receive in kind, and that he'd give her whatever support she needed to help her feel better about her body.

Justin was surprised by other items on Kris's list, such as dressing up in costumes. "I'd love it if you'd wear a policeman's costume and rescue me," Kris said, smiling mischievously. "I also know you watch porn and would love it if you'd share one of your favorites with me. And one more thing. I wonder if we could go to an erotic boutique and pick up some restraints. I want to take turns tying up our hands."

Justin's eyes nearly popped out of his head. "Let's do it!" he exclaimed.

Kris was surprised by how much Justin's menu was devoted to non-genital activities. "I love being touched," Justin said shyly. "The more the better: a neck rub, a hand massage, a back rub. I love holding hands with you and spooning on the couch. I'd love it if you would come up behind me and hug me." He paused. "I'd also love it if you'd tell me all the ways I'm attractive to you."

After sharing the individual menus, I asked them to go home, discuss the items from each list that both were willing to try, and create a joint sexual menu. Any activities that didn't make the list would be put on a separate "to be explored" menu that we'd revisit after their sexual reconnection was in full gear.

In the next session they presented their combined sexual menu, which they read aloud together. They organized items by senses: visual (undressing in front of each other, viewing porn, dressing up in costumes, watching a sunset while holding each other); auditory (reading erotic stories out loud in bed, talking dirty); smell (massaging each other with scented oils, making love after exercising without showering); taste (Kris licks chocolate sauce off Justin's penis, they make special meals together and eat them in bed naked), and touch (holding hands, spooning, genital massages). They sat close together and giggled throughout their menu report. I reminded them that their menu is a work in progress, changeable over time. But they barely heard me, they were laughing so hard. I knew the process of co-creating safe potential space (Winnicott, 1971) had begun where playful exploration was possible.

The Sexual Menu and Trauma

When one of the partners has suffered trauma in the past, such as sexual abuse, assault, or rape, I suggest that the survivor construct an initial sexual menu that excludes items that are triggering, upsetting, or uncomfortable. For example, someone may find it triggering to be penetrated from behind because it has associations with rape. Their sexual menu will exclude that item. If a survivor isn't clear about what triggers him/her/them, I often incorporate bibliotherapy to begin educating him/her/them (and the partner) about how sexual abuse can affect sexuality. A helpful resource is *The Sexual Healing Journey* by Wendy Maltz (1991).

Some trauma survivors feel safer creating a menu alone with me initially. Such was the case with a man named Ted who had been terribly abused by his psychotic mother and was very shut down sexually. Ted felt too uncomfortable discussing the menu with his girlfriend present, even though I told him he could share only those things he was comfortable sharing. The big issue with survivors is control. Control of their bodies was taken away from them, so I err on the side of giving as much control as I can to the person, including how sexual exercises are done.

In working with trauma, I start very small. One couple I worked with never had intercourse because of past trauma. They developed a menu that had low trigger potential, such as non-genital massages without leading to orgasm or oral sex. Other couples shower together, sometimes with bathing suits on at first.

Once couples are utilizing the sexual menu for a while, I'll ask if they want to revisit the list of menu items that weren't included. They're generally more ready to explore those possibilities at this point because they feel safer and erotically connected. They now view themselves as sexually functional rather than dysfunctional, and can more freely discuss the more difficult or "kinkier" sexual items. Maybe one of them wants to be tied up. Or perhaps they want to try role-plays or even a threesome.

As couples become increasingly connected, it's rewarding to see how their narratives change. They become freer and more open with one another. Their guilt and shame are greatly reduced. The troublesome sexual narratives they've always told themselves begin to change. In a sense, they've begun creating a new sexual history.

Sometimes the sexual menu will reveal what seem like stark differences between the partners. One person's menu might be mostly genital sexual, while the other person's is sensual non-physical, like walks on the beach or eating strawberries together. I can hear clients saying, "See, your list has no touching. You never want me. We're not compatible."

Sexual differences in couples can be a good thing. Instead of being incompatible, differences can be complementary. If couples combine their sexual interests, they're covering a lot of territory. They can visit all the Chinese and Italian restaurants in town for tasting menus or full-course meals. They can bring elements of sensuality and sexuality together by learning from each other and teaching each other. And that can only make their sex life better than it's ever been before.

CHAPTER 5

※

MOVING FROM MIND TO BODY
A Narrative Approach to Mindful Touch

Our inner narratives fly through our minds at lightning speed and collide with our sex lives without us even realizing it. To put people more in touch with enjoying the physical experience of sex, I teach them an array of mindfulness techniques (Hahn, 1992; Kabat-Zinn, 1994) to slow down their thoughts so they can be present in the moment during erotic encounters with self and others. This helps return them to the intensity and immediacy of their sexual experiences and diminishes the power of the stories that get in the way of connection, arousal, and sexual satisfaction. Mindfulness helps people develop a capacity for presence, which is the capacity to rest in an experience fully, with whatever is going on physically and emotionally. Recent studies show that long-term couples who have a highly satisfying erotic relationship describe a sense of presence as one of the major components of sexual experiences.

To teach mindfulness, I use a modified version of Masters and Johnson's Sensate Focus. Sensate Focus involved partners touching each other for short periods of time, moving through a progression from non-erogenous parts to erogenous parts and then on to penetrative sex and intercourse. The goal of sensate focus exercises is to move steadily from levels of touch toward intercourse. (For a comprehensive description of Masters and Johnson's Sensate Focus Technique, see Weiner & Avery-Clark [2017].)

Masters and Johnson believed that a primary source of sexual dysfunction was *spectatoring*, which they defined as observing what one is doing instead of experiencing it. Sensate focus or progressive touching emphasizes attending to physical sensation instead of one's thoughts. It is often prescribed to break the ice and set in motion a progressive process of physical engagement.

Instead of attempting to banish the "observer," I welcome it as an ally in helping each partner discover what distracts them during sexual engagement.

Unlike Masters and Johnson, I use sensate focus to help clients become aware of mind/body narratives that disrupt sexual presence and pleasure. Using meditation techniques, I ask clients to become aware of their thoughts, feelings, bodily sensations, and breathing while touching.

Becoming Aware of "The Noise in the Head"

If clients are not acquainted with meditation, I begin with a simple exercise in a session. For example, I ask clients to close their eyes, breathe slowly, and just be aware of what goes on inside themselves for one minute of clock time. After a minute I ring a meditation chime and ask them to slowly open their eyes and return to the room. Then I ask them to report what they noticed — thoughts, feelings, or sensations in their bodies. I normalize the "*noise in the head*" that exists in everyone in greater or lesser amounts at any given time, and emphasize that it's not the presence of the noise that's often problematic during sex but what we do with it — believe it, get distracted by it, stop having sex because of it. I tell clients that the more they practice short meditations at home, the less disruptive the "noise in the head" will become. I often assign meditation as part of sex therapy. Apps like *Headspace, Breethe*, and *Calm* are particularly helpful for structuring meditation sessions at home.

I don't use mindful touch in a linear, progressive way, as many sex therapists do, starting with non-erogenous zones and moving toward penetrative sex. I've found that type of progressive approach can increase anxiety because people are thinking about the endpoint instead of being in the present moment. I teach mindful touch with no predetermined endpoint, certainly not one predetermined by me.

The mindfulness part of satisfying sexuality is often overlooked by clients and therapists, but it is truly important. Too often, *the mind is not our friend when it comes to sex*. I often tell clients that when people are struggling with sex, usually their mind is saying something fraught or unkind. We discover our "noisy minds" when we meditate. It can be terrifying to realize how much we talk to ourselves every second, and how much of that inner monologue can be negative, anxious, repetitive, or fixated on past or future, the perfect definition of self-defeating.

That inner monologue is on steroids when people have sex. Our sexual histories are on full display, and it's rare when we don't have a nagging commentary going on in the background. Most of us are not aware of the content of that inner noise and how it affects us sexually, how thought can interfere with the body and become a barrier to feeling present and satisfied with a partner.

Through mindful touch, clients become aware of what they're thinking as they're either touching or being touched. The point of mindful touch is to de-center genital sex as the primary way to connect sexually by starting with small physical steps to connect. This helps clients start to become aware of the noise in their heads.

In teaching this approach, I suggest "containers" to provide safety and predictability for partners while exploring mindful touch. I borrow this concept from psychoanalyst Wilfred Bion (1962), who discussed the power of containment, which conveys a sense of safety where people can move through emotions together. One of the containers I use is time. I ask couples to start with five minutes of giving and receiving mindful touch. That can be a long time, depending on the couple's sexual history. For a trauma survivor, being present sexually for that amount of time might be a real challenge. In such a case, touching can take place for two minutes or even less.

Mindful touch is not the same as massage. The point is not to help one's partner with a tight neck or tense shoulders. Mindful touch is *slow touch done with a flat hand*, which is much more intimate than massage because there's no goal or script involved. The point is to slow down and experience the sensation and intimacy of giving and receiving touch.

I instruct clients not to touch erogenous zones – no contact with breasts, nipples, genitals, or anus. Some people add to this list, such as the inside of their thighs or their necks. If someone is dealing with sexual problems, like erectile issues or painful intercourse, touching the genitals can initially feel quite fraught, especially if one's internalized sexual model is based on arousal and orgasm.

I also instruct clients to purchase a journal just for the purpose of these exercises to write down their experiences with touching and being touched. Writing serves as another container. I ask them to write answers to the following questions:

"What were the thoughts?"
"What were the feelings?"
"What was I sensing in the body?"

As clients write these answers about giving and receiving touch in their journals, over time they begin to identify patterns that comprise their unique body narratives.

I tell clients that there are no right or wrong answers to these questions. I normalize "noise in the mind" by saying, "Your mind will be noisy unless you've been practicing yoga or meditation for twenty-five years." Most clients have minimal experience with meditation. I encourage them not to judge that noise. Rather, I ask them to be curious about what it's saying to them and how it's affecting them.

When clients finish their writing, I tell them not to talk about the touching or read their notes to each other. In the beginning the risk of self-criticism or criticism of their partner is too great. They should bring their journals to the next session, where they will read their writing out loud and share how their adventure in giving and receiving touch this week turned out. There of course is no "failed" experience. We learn from whatever happens.

When the couple comes in for their next appointment with me, they each read their notes. They identify the thoughts (the "noise") they were having. That "noise" might have important content that needs to be explored. One person might be saying to him/her/themself, "Oh, I can't believe we're reduced to this silly touching exercise." The other person may be saying to him/her/themself, "My body is too fat. How could my partner possibly like me?" These kinds of negative thoughts could be directed at the self or at the partner.

Like with non-touch, meditation thoughts are not judged, just noticed. There is no right or wrong thought. The important thing is to be aware of one's relationship to one's thoughts. Over time, those thoughts change, becoming less noisy. This is what makes mindful narrative touching a non-progressive activity. It's not progressive, like in sensate focus, touching toward the goal of penetrative sex. The focus, rather, is non-linear – being present in the moment and noticing one's thoughts.

Some couples stay with the five-minute touching limit for months. Sometimes they gradually expand the time limit on their own and become less dependent on me for guidance. They may move on to touching other parts of the body or erogenous zones.

For instance, some couples will decide to shower together and soap each other. They may move into genital touch, perhaps just cupping the penis or the vulva for a short amount of time, with the emphasis on mindfulness and being present.

Sometimes I'll assign what's called a soft penis massage. Borrowed from Tantric sex practices that focus more on presence than performance, the goal is not to get the penis hard, but to slow down and merely experience the sensation of the partner's hand on one's soft penis. I also advise the receiver that even if you get hard or excited, don't move so fast. Don't make orgasm the endpoint. Make sensation, presence, and connection the endpoint. In the meantime, be curious what the body is saying, the soft penis in this case. I reframe the soft penis as an ally in healing, that is communicating what needs to be heard by the client. Perhaps the soft penis is saying, "It is not safe to show up in this relationship" or "I am too angry to give you pleasure by being hard." The body narratives can be connected to childhood experiences and/or those associated with the present relationship. (For more information on erotic healing touch, see The New School of Erotic Touch at www.erotic massage.com.)

Eventually, if they feel comfortable, a couple can move on to more interactive experiences. There is no predetermined endpoint, and I don't suggest one. Couples take on more control as they feel safer with each other, as their communication skills improve, and as their criticism of self and other is reduced. Their sexuality becomes less fraught and more expansive, linked to willingness and not necessarily desire.

For couples who've been concerned about their sexual lives for years, ignoring the mind is not easy. Instructions, in traditional sensate focus, to focus on sensation bypassing thoughts and feelings, usually ends up with clients feeling defeated. After years of sexual deprivation, frustration, performance anxiety, or failure, it often seems impossible to rid the mind/body of its associations to childhood trauma, past wounds, or fearful outcomes. Distracting thoughts combined with concerns about "what's supposed to happen next" often cause clients to avoid the assignment or eventually lose interest as a defense. I should say here that some couples I've worked with can indeed follow the traditional sensate focus method of bypassing thoughts and feelings by focusing on sensation. But, most couples I've worked with do not progress at some point unless they process past trauma and wounds contained within their mind/body narratives.

With these couples, I structure exercises by introducing parameters for safety: preplanning the time and place for touching, how long it will last (using a timer), how much clothing will be worn, what parts of the body are okay to include, and how to ask for a time-out. Partners also decide whether they want to touch each other in back-to-back experiences or at separate times during the week.

Mindful touch was very helpful for Kris and Justin. "Become more aware and curious about what your minds have to say about giving and receiving bodily pleasure," I told them. "You'll gradually let go of thoughts as you become less reactive to your inner noise." And finally, I said, "As you give and receive touch, remember to breathe."

During this exercise, Kris wasn't surprised by her thoughts, which harped non-stop on her inadequacies as she touched Justin, but she was shocked by how much "louder" these judgments seemed when she was on the receiving end of a sexual encounter. Having had few partners before Justin, she'd long experienced performance anxiety about how to pleasure a man. She now realized that she suffered more response anxiety than performance anxiety, which she associated with not being good enough to keep her father home or make her mother happy.

Meanwhile, Justin's inner noise was finely tuned to his perception of Kris's degree of sexual pleasure. If she was clearly enjoying herself, or if he knew how to shift his approach to please her more, his mind was quieter. He felt in control of the situation. But if he couldn't tell how Kris was feeling, he was flooded with anxiety. The sense of uncertainty, he realized, hearkened back to the charged calm before his father's storms. No amount of vigilance or effort could prevent them.

Justin and Kris began to realize how the yin/yang of their mind/body narratives triggered each other. The more vigilant Justin became when sexually anxious, the more Kris felt scrutinized. The more scrutinized she felt, the less responsive she became, further ratcheting up Justin's uncertainty and fear. As they became more aware of their inner noise through observation, writing, and sharing, the cacophony gradually diminished, allowing them to be more present with each other when giving and receiving touch. "It feels safer now," Kris said. "We keep trying out new things, even ones that feel a bit scary."

In a sense, mindful narrative touch helps retrain people's bodies in how to be physically intimate without assumptions, preconditions, or goals, an essential step in rewriting negative sexual narratives, especially those associated with challenging sexual experiences.

PART 2

APPLYING NRST TO CHALLENGING SEXUAL ISSUES

CHAPTER 6

※

EMBRACING THE COMPLEXITY OF
SEXUALITY

Sex is a queer experience for everyone at one time or another. It can be unruly, ecstatic, routine, mysterious, joyous, transgressive, disturbing, confusing, unpredictable, and changeable over one's lifetime. Sexuality is highly complex, defying easy generalization, categorization, and explanation.

Most of us think of "queer experience" as relating to gay or lesbian experience or as gender non-conforming experience. I use the term "queer" here in three much broader ways:

- First, it reminds us of the potential fluidity and multidimensionality of same, in-between, and other sex/gender experience in all people. Even Freud said that we all have the inherent capacity for bisexuality, whether in thought, feeling, or deed.
- Second, "queer experience" embodies the confounding nature of sexuality in general, with its incongruities and paradoxes in identities, behaviors, attractions, thoughts, feelings, fantasies, and sensations.
- Finally, for therapists reading this book, it normalizes our awkwardness in working with clients as our cherished beliefs and assumptions about sexuality and gender are challenged.

In looking at the complexity of sex, Rosemary Basson's work suggests "real" (binary) gender differences with regard to sexuality, but it's important to remember that there can be significant within-group differences. Helpful here are the thoughts of relational psychoanalysts Adrienne Harris and Jody Davies.

Harris, in her book *Gender as Soft Assembly* (2005), offers a vision of gender as consisting of "shifting constructions" and everyday "contradictions," instead of stable binary categories. She encourages us to think of our sexuality in a

87

subjective way, as including multiple gendered and embodied selves that are configured within multiple contexts over the lifespan. Jody Davies (2006) discusses the capacity for multiple erotic "self-states" – parts of the self that can access different parts of our personality. This isn't like multiple personality disorder; it's entirely normal for someone to have different self-states. Self-states are parts of self that feel authentic to the person and are very important to one's identity, even if sometimes they seem incongruent.

In my work with diverse clients – gay, lesbian, bisexual, heterosexual, trans – I have often observed how varied "gendered" experiences or self-states can co-exist within the individual, depending on context, relational dynamics, or sexual activities, that for some clients, and therapists, feel uncomfortably "queer." I will give an illustration of this in the upcoming case of Harold and Martha.

Conflictual feelings about certain self-states during sex can limit erotic enjoyment. An example would be a person in a peer relationship, which I discussed in detail in Chapter 1, who feels great pride and identification in sharing power equally with their partner outside the bedroom – in the kitchen, raising the kids, and managing careers and finances. But in the bedroom, sexual passion is better served by self-states involving unequal power where one partner might want to dominate or be dominated by the other. When each partner shifts from one self-state to another, both self-states (equality and powerplay) are equally authentic, true parts representing the complexities of the self.

For some people, the inability to shift or integrate certain self-states can be related to societal factors. For example, some men struggle with playing with power, especially now in the context of the #MeToo movement. They're wary about shifting into aggressive self-states in the bedroom. A fair number of these men identify as feminists and are appalled at the idea that they could be seen as sexual perpetrators by abusing power or being seen as coercive, especially with female partners. They would rather err on the side of caution instead of risking a behavior that could be viewed as inappropriate. They don't allow themselves the flexibility to shift into a different self-state, even if a female partner openly desires a more aggressive approach in the bedroom. Many men don't know the difference between being assertive, aggressive, or coercive and need to examine those differences in therapy.

Another example applies to some lesbians who came of age sexually during the women's rights movement in the 1960s and '70s. Some avoided penetrative sex because they viewed it as mimicking heterosexual patriarchy. Or, they wouldn't participate in powerplay sex, like BDSM, or use porn.

Being a good feminist and a hot sexual couple were incompatible if it meant practicing sexual activities containing unequal power roles. On the other hand, pro-porn, pro-BDSM lesbian feminists argued that they felt policed and restrained by "sex-negative" feminists. On a community level, these conflicting narratives created a painful period in the 1980s, called the Sex Wars, tearing at the fabric of the larger feminist community. On a couple level, avoiding "politically incorrect sex" contributed to many lesbian couples losing desire or not having sex at all either because the sex felt restricted or because partners felt shame about certain sexual desires. The main source of the challenges in these examples were external – in the socio-political environment of the time.

Creating Safe Therapeutic Space for the Complexity of Sexuality

In many cases, sexual challenges like these can be understood and transformed through the use of *externalization of the problem* that helps clients realize how societal or community narratives become internalized, creating conflict and shame within individuals and between partners. This is tender work. Challenging complex internalized sexual narratives requires the therapist to construct a safe enough therapeutic container within which shamed, wounded, and disowned parts of the self can be revealed, worked through, and integrated. How does a therapist construct such a safe container?

From the beginning of therapy, I create a safe potential erotic space (Iasenza, 2004) by inquiring about, exploring, mirroring, and, if necessary, normalizing and reframing complex "queer" sexual experiences. Winnicott (1971) discussed his approach to developing an inviting potential space where children may trust the relational environment enough to play creatively. In this case, the therapist can begin earning trust by curiously and non-judgmentally inquiring about the client's sexual complexities from his/her/their point of view.

Some of the deepest empathic work occurs during individual sexual history sessions. Queer experiences may be conscious or unconscious, openly discussed, or hidden sources of sexual difficulty. Some clients experience distress about the fluidity of same, in-between, and other sex/gender experience, or about incongruities in their sexual identities, behavior, attractions, thoughts, feelings, fantasies, and sensations. Through therapeutic sexual history-taking, we can begin to gently identify and deconstruct assumptions about sexuality.

What this requires is that we all (both clients and therapists) learn to tolerate "queer moments" about sexuality – when we feel perplexed, off balance, or uncomfortable with the intensities and surprises that can show up in a therapy session. It's especially important that therapists prepare for "queer moments" in therapy, so they may best handle feeling triggered or dysregulated. How do we deal with queer (or potentially queasy) therapy moments, when feelings of repulsion, boredom, excitement, confusion, or surprise emerge when discussing sexuality?

Here are some examples of possible revelations in therapy that can produce queer moments:

- Having sexual feelings for both men and women
- Feeling one's assigned sex doesn't match one's experience of gender
- Being happy with one's assigned sex but wanting to be socially experienced as someone of the other sex, or as non-gendered
- Sexual attraction to someone who is trans or genderqueer
- Not identifying as either gender
- Not able to desire the person who one loves
- Never having experienced sexual desire in one's life
- Never having experienced sexual attraction in one's life
- Only enjoying sex when imagining oneself as the other gender
- Having sexual fantasies about disturbing things
- Being heterosexually married and having an affair with someone of the same sex
- Being a lesbian who has sex with men
- Being a gay man who fantasizes about women when having sex
- Being someone who likes physical pain with sex
- Being a man who likes to wear women's clothing
- Being a heterosexual man who desires anal penetration
- Becoming sexually excited by being humiliated
- Experiencing sexual arousal from objects (e.g., stockings, leather) or particular body parts (e.g., feet)

The list can go on and on. Increased accessibility to sexual images and practices through the internet has made the discovery of and indulgence in queer sexual experiences much easier for people in recent times.

Yet sexuality and gender remain loaded issues in our culture, within families, and for individuals and couples. The fact that few of us – therapists and the general public alike – receive any in-depth education about human sexuality only adds to the problem.

Couple therapists are not required to have any training in sexuality. Esther Perel, author of *Mating in Captivity*, said in a *New York Times* interview (Sohn, 2015) that she received just one hour of education about sex in her psychotherapy training. And today, there is just one certification program for sex therapists, offered by the American Association of Sexuality Educators, Counselors and Therapists (AASECT). Short of pursuing formal sex therapy training, therapists can prepare for uneasy "queer" moments by reading and viewing diverse sexual materials, discussing sexuality issues with colleagues at professional conferences or in case consultations, and participating in peer or facilitated study groups. A good rule of thumb is: if something feels "ick" by just thinking about it, it's worth learning more about it.

The Case of Harold and Martha: Encountering Queerness in a Relationship

The case of Harold and Martha illustrates how the experience of "queer sexuality" can disrupt a couple's relationship, and how the NRST process can help address these kinds of obstacles when they arise.

Harold and Martha, a couple in their fifties who had been married for five years, entered sex therapy to understand why their sexual life began to fizzle after their first year of marriage. This problem confused them, given their passionate twelve-month "honeymoon period" and a longstanding mutual sexual attraction. Other than their avoidance of sex, they thought their relationship was strong, describing it as highly affectionate, companionable, and enjoyable. Having no children enabled them to indulge in an active life of travel, sports, and cultural events.

Harold was a handsome, six-foot-tall, ex-college football star; he now worked as a businessman. He had had many sexual conquests in his youth that bolstered his manly self-image. Yet despite his sexual success, Harold had few long-term relationships, and his first marriage ended sadly when his wife left him. Martha, attractive and slightly built, was a successful investment banker. She also knew heartbreak when her first husband left her for another woman. A Phi Beta Kappa graduate of an Ivy League college, Martha said she never felt sex appeal was her strength. Although she had few sexual relationships, she always liked sex.

I asked them how they defined "sex" and what sexual response model they worked from (performance-based, pleasure-based, or connection-based). They laughed and admitted that they were driven people in business and in bed, and their sex reflected it. They felt compatible in their routine, with Harold initiating kissing, touching, and intercourse. Both masturbated occasionally. They never discussed sex.

Harold and Martha's treatment goal was to increase sexual frequency. The catalyst for coming to therapy was the divorce of their closest married friend. They feared if sex didn't return to their relationship, they might not be able to stay together. When I explained my need to see them separately to conduct sexual histories, they readily agreed and set up separate appointments for the following week.

A Disturbing "Different Gender" Experience

When Harold arrived for his first individual session, he seemed sheepish. He acknowledged his lack of experience in talking about sex apart from typical boasting with male peers. The middle of three boys, he attributed his silence about sex to his ex-Marine father's stoic toughness and his mother's genteel WASP style. His early childhood experiences were unremarkable to him. His earliest sexual memory was playing doctor with neighborhood kids. He reported no memories of shame or boundary transgressions. Throughout the session, Harold commented about my nonchalant style in talking about sex. He expressed amazement and appreciation that such an open conversation was possible. I grew curious about Harold's expression of these feelings and wondered if they held some deeper meaning for him.

It wasn't until the middle of his second individual sexual history session that the reason for Harold's appreciation revealed itself. I asked him why his first marriage ended. He painfully confessed that it was his fault. Halfway through his ten-year marriage, he periodically began losing erections, forcing him to change his typical sexual script, consisting of initiation and intercourse, to one consisting of more expansive foreplay. When in the receptive role, he became aware of heightened arousal when his wife played with his nipples and poked his anus. What disturbed him was an accompanying fantasy where his wife became a female top (the dominant partner) with him the female bottom (receptive partner), his penis transformed into a throbbing clitoris, her finger in his anus becoming a dildo entering his fantasy vagina.

"I felt like I was having lesbian sex with my wife, for God's sake. I must be a perv," Harold exclaimed in embarrassment, "and I stopped it by withdrawing from sex."

This unexpected disclosure created a queer moment for me that I handled by taking a breath and putting myself into Harold's queer experience, wondering what further meaning it held for him. I then asked, "What do you think is most challenging for you about that experience?"

Harold sat in silence for a while. Then he smiled and said, "This is just one more aspect of my sexuality to explore, isn't it?"

"Yes," I replied, "it's not so unusual for people to experience different gendered states, especially during sex."

Harold talked about feeling torn between feeling ashamed of his fantasy and attracted to it. He was afraid of how it might ruin his relationship with Martha. His masturbatory fantasies only consisted of heterosexual sex.

We tried to understand the beginnings of his new fantasy and wondered if his lack of desire for Martha supported its development or vice versa. I wondered aloud to Harold if his strict intercourse script was more of a defense against vulnerability than a preference. He willingly let himself wonder about that and shared how painful it was to see his gentle mother endure his father's overbearing ways.

"Perhaps I'm a man torn between acting dominant like my father," he told me, "and preferring the gentleness of my mother. I really felt for her even though I never let on about it."

I told Harold that it wasn't a surprise that his fantasy showed up within a committed relationship, where most people's internalized wishes, fears, and conflicts from childhood re-emerge. I added, "You couldn't keep up the dominant role with your ex-wife, and you can't do it now with Martha. Being committed long-term often requires embracing vulnerability, and your lesbian experience exists to help you accept and integrate that part."

Harold was intrigued by this alternative narrative and said he would think about it.

An Early Experience of Rejection and Shame

Martha's sexual history revealed a narrative where she didn't feel desired as an attractive woman. Her older sister Jane was a "prom queen type" favored by both her parents. Jane bonded with their mom around domestic activities

(Martha was a tomboy), and their dad showered Jane with compliments about her looks and popularity. Martha felt like the ugly duckling loner at home. She excelled at sports with boys in the neighborhood, which contributed to her confidence and skill in competing in a male-dominated career later in life. She married late, at age forty, to a man who devastated her by having several affairs. "He told me my best asset was my mind. I felt like a failure as a woman."

When Martha met Harold at a party, she felt like "the sexiest woman in the room from the way he looked at me. He was surrounded at the bar by several attractive women, and he left the party with me. I felt like my time had finally arrived."

After a short courtship, they married and Martha had high hopes of fulfilling her dream of romance. Sex was wonderful at first, but as Martha perceived Harold's gradual retreat from sex, her feelings of failure as a woman painfully resurfaced: "I feel it every day."

I said to her, "I imagine the pain goes way back to when you felt so rejected and alone in your family."

"Yes," she said sadly. "I used to feel so ashamed when my father complimented Jane right in front of me, as if something was wrong with me."

"And how did you deal with it then?" I asked.

"The same as I do now — I retreat," Martha said. As I finished her sexual history, I realized that her sensitivity to rejection and her desire to feel desired outweighed any particular preference regarding sexual activities or roles. Although she relied mostly on intercourse, she was open to a greater variety of sexual experiences, including oral and anal sensuality, and foreplay involving breast/nipple play, and sensual touch.

Harold and Martha were suffering from a sexless marriage caused by false narratives, shameful secrets, and painful defenses and re-enactments stemming from their childhoods. These problems were compounded by poor communication skills. Harold's shame and conflict about his "queerness" (and the vulnerability it represented and created) caused him to withdraw from sex, triggering Martha's feelings of rejection and failure as a woman. To cope she retreated, intensifying Harold's fear that his queerness would ruin their relationship. Such sexual yin/yangs are common in committed relationships.

Harold and Martha's strengths included their continued sexual attraction to each other and their companionable relationship, which I hoped could be tapped as a resource during subsequent sexual assignments.

Reframing Sexual Problems Through NRST

In the session following the completion of sexual histories, I share parts of each person's history (with their prior permission), for the purpose of opening discussion and fostering understanding about their sexual problem. I reframe sexual problems as an opportunity for growth. I tell clients: "Oftentimes our most difficult sexual issues contain parts of our past experiences, conscious or unconscious, that are unresolved. As we work together, we will identify what past experiences are playing out for each of you now."

I usually ask couples if they shared any of their sexual history discussions with each other. I wasn't surprised to hear that Harold and Martha hadn't, and I used that as an example about how little they communicated with each other, especially about sexual feelings and experiences. I pointed out how neither of them witnessed open and constructive communication in their families. Both had learned about sex outside of the home. I also pointed out how their vulnerabilities as children had been denied in the family, Harold's as it related to his mother's (and his own) vulnerability to his father's dominance, and Martha's experience of her parents' preference for her sister.

I suggested to Harold and Martha that they ran their early sexual life like a successful business – efficient, predictable, and performance-based. Such an approach might be enjoyable at first but was unsustainable over the long haul. I asked them if they'd be willing to experiment with other approaches to sex that are more pleasure or connection-based, so they could slow down and learn to communicate better with each other. They agreed.

I prescribed a vacation from intercourse, which prompted their laughter since they hadn't attempted sex in almost a year.

Deconstructing Sex With the Sexual Menu

Part of co-creating new sexual experiences involves a process of deconstructing sex and increasing sexual communication. Many "sexless" relationships develop because a couple has a one-item sexual menu. Such was the case with Harold and Martha. If one partner doesn't want to have intercourse, a sexual invitation gets turned down, and sometimes the kissing and hugging stops as well. The problem is that the sexual menu is very limited and allows no chance for flexibility in the bedroom.

When I gave Harold and Martha the sexual menu assignment, I instructed each of them to make a list of everything they could think of that was sexual, sensual, or erotic. I encouraged them not to censor themselves by labeling an item as too tame, kinky, or queer. Forget what their partner likes or dislikes – there are no "good" or "bad," "right" or "wrong" menu items. Lists can be neither too long nor too short, and may be revised.

When they returned the following week, Harold and Martha told me that just compiling their lists expanded their awareness of many pleasurable erotic activities beyond intercourse.

I asked each to share his/her list with no cross-talk. Given their lack of sexual communication, I told them that many people feel embarrassed or awkward when reading their lists out loud, so it was okay if they felt those feelings. I then invited them to discuss their reactions to each other's list, being mindful to use non-critical language.

The menu paved the way for Harold to raise his desire for nipple and anal play, as he casually mentioned them among other possible items he preferred. He appeared relieved that Martha seemed to have no particular antipathy toward them, something he had always feared. I knew this represented the beginning of a profound healing for Harold.

Martha's list included relational items, like flirting and being picked up at a bar, which spoke to her need to feel desired again by Harold. Neither felt surprised or uncomfortable with any of their partner's items. Both welcomed the opportunity to learn more about each other. I asked them to create a larger couple sexual menu consisting of agreed-upon items from their individual menus, but since they hadn't been sexually intimate for a while, we would start with touching.

Narrative Mindful Touch

I asked Harold and Martha to begin (non-erogenous zone) touching for just five minutes each and to use a timer instead of looking at a clock. They decided to start with clothes on. I asked each of them to keep a sexual journal to write about their experiences after giving and receiving. I told them to refrain from sharing their writing or verbally processing the experience at home. They would do so in session. Over the next few months, they increased the time spent touching and removed more of their clothing.

Harold was surprised by how long it took him to settle down mentally. His *inner noise* was greater when he received; this made sense, since his lifelong sexual script was about being the dominant giver. He felt much more vulnerable as the receiver.

Martha became aware that her fears of rejection were much more present when she gave than when she received. She assumed that if Harold was giving to her, it meant that he desired her. Her fears even extended to initiating the writing assignment. Harold, as he did in their sexual relationship, usually initiated it. These insights opened up a deeper discussion about how each of them struggled with different narratives related to desiring or being desired.

Over the next several weeks, Harold told Martha how much he wanted her whenever she gave to him, so she could experience herself as desirable in that role. Martha encouraged Harold to practice asking to have different body parts touched so he could feel safer as the receiver. It was very moving to see how Harold and Martha were beginning to become healers of each other's deepest wounds. By identifying persistent distracting thoughts, Harold and Martha were able to work through underlying narratives, and eventually the distractions subsided. They became grounded in their bodies in more expansive ways. The structure of this assignment, including time limits and writing, created a safe way for them to explore their erotic potential through touch.

As couples feel more competent, they take ownership of therapy assignments (length, content, and frequency), eventually bringing a mindful presence and renewed passion to expansive sexual experiences. I knew Harold and Martha experienced a breakthrough when, after including erogenous zones for several weeks, they reported that Martha confidently initiated the assignment and Harold asked Martha to concentrate on his nipples. She loved giving him pleasure and he loved receiving it. He was fully aroused and expressed his desire for her. Their healing was happening.

Normalizing the Complex Realm of Fantasy

Helen Singer Kaplan said that all sex requires is the two F's – fantasy and friction. Sex is where the body and the mind connect.

When we look at how we experience sexual pleasure, we start with the physical, because that's how we experience sensual pleasure developmentally, starting in infancy. As we grow older, sex becomes more than a physical experience as we enter the realm of the mind through imagination and fantasy.

Michael Bader (2002) explores the intriguing world of people's sexual fantasies in *Arousal: The Secret Logic of Sexual Fantasies*. Nancy Friday (1973) broke ground by writing about women's fantasies in *My Secret Garden* at the height of the women's movement. Both emphasize the incredible variety of sexual fantasies and how fantasy life can be a resource beyond what we experience on solely a physical level. Bader additionally presents a psychoanalytic perspective about the psychological meaning and possible healing power of sexual fantasies, like we saw with Harold's lesbian fantasy.

Some people when they masturbate are aroused by the physical sensation alone. Touching is enough to bring them to orgasm. Their focus is on the sensory experience instead of fantasy. Other people require fantasy, some relying on the same fantasy over and over. They may also use porn or erotica for stimulation and may get aroused with little physical contact. It's helpful to educate clients about these different approaches to self-pleasure. For some people the mind is really the driving force; for other people it's the body. One is not better than the other.

A major challenge for many clients is to understand their fantasies in a non-judgmental way. Many people struggle with their fantasies and need to work through fear or shame about them. It is helpful to distinguish fantasy from behavior. If one fantasizes about having sex with children, it doesn't mean that one will act on it, although it is important for therapists to inquire about sexual behavior in this instance to ensure the protection of children. Women who imagine being raped don't want that in reality. Underlying the fantasy may be a desire to let go of control, or as in old romance novels, to be sexually swept away. Many times therapists are the first to hear about secret shameful or confusing fantasies during sexual history sessions. It is important to explore what the fantasies mean, help the client reduce shame about them, and examine how they may be affecting the client's sexual/relational life.

In conducting a client's sexual history, I ask about masturbation history, favorite fantasies, and porn use. I explore fantasies and porn like I explore dreams. If someone has a favorite kind of porn or a favorite fantasy, I engage the client to become curious about "Why that particular scene?". My goal, as always, is not to judge or change the fantasy/porn preference, but to understand it within the context of the person's sexual and relational history. Why does someone fantasize about being held down by three men? Perhaps he doesn't want to take responsibility for his sexual desires. Why does another person fantasize about seducing everyone in the room? Perhaps they never felt sexually attractive. What purpose does the fantasy serve in the person's interior life? How is it an attempt to heal old wounds?

Robert Stoller (1979) suggests that sexual excitement inevitably contains an unconscious expression of aggression in the form of revenge against a person(s) who, in early life, made some form of threat to the child's core identity, either in the form of overt trauma or through the psychological frustrations and wounds of childhood development. He argued that all types of sexual expression, not just kinky or non-normative sexuality, contain an attempt to work through early conflict, an attempt at mastery of past trauma. How well was your gender identity embraced by your family of origin? Did your parents accept your erotic yearnings? Or did you split off those yearnings because you were made to feel they were inappropriate? Were you an Oedipal victor, where one parent preferred you over the other? Or did you feel excluded from the parental couple? What narratives about sexuality and relationships did these experiences create?

The world of sexual fantasies gives us clues. Rather than certain fantasies being seen as perverted or abnormal, they can be appreciated for their educational value about a client's inner life. This is often a very comforting view. Most clients, when they hear this, breathe a big sigh of relief. So many clients I encounter in my practice feel weighed down by the worry that they're more dysfunctional or perverted than the average person. I often remind them that sexual preferences and fantasies serve a valuable function beyond just pleasure.

Using NRST to Work With Sexual Fantasies

When I train therapists and tell them to ask clients about their sexual fantasies, I often get a nervous reaction from them: "Oh my God, what do I say when someone shares a masturbation fantasy or a sexual dream?"

I tell them it's no different than if someone brought in a "regular dream" to therapy: you ask them about it. You listen to them and then say, "Well, why do you think that male figure is in your dream? Is that your father? A part of you? Your partner? What is the dream saying?"

With a sexual fantasy, the questions are no different: "What is the fantasy saying?"

The Case of Casey's Disturbing Sexual Fantasy as Relational Mastery

I saw a lesbian client, Casey, who was very disturbed by a fantasy she had while masturbating. What threw her over the edge was imagining that she was being gang-banged by a group of men.

She found this appalling on a number of levels. She had never had sex with men, having always been attracted to and involved with women. Was she becoming bisexual? Was she "not really gay"? These questions troubled her, although it's not uncommon for people to have sexual fantasies or experiences that are incongruent with their sexual identities. She was especially haunted by the violence of the fantasy – and most of all because as she was held down and serially raped, she was enjoying it.

Why would she enjoy being coerced and abused? And in public, nonetheless? When I asked her if she would have felt less upset if the fantasy had involved only one man, she agreed. What was disturbing was the group nature of the violation, with some of the men masturbating while they watched her being raped. She had never had group sex. The fantasy made her question not only her sexual orientation but also her sexual health. Was she a masochist? Did she secretly crave violent sex?

It's helpful for therapists to view any sexual or masturbatory fantasy through the framework of dream analysis. Guide the client away from a literal interpretation of the fantasy and toward understanding the symbolism of the fantasy and what the various figures/themes in it represent. The first step is not to draw concrete conclusions but to open up an exploration. Like with dreams, there could be several levels of interpretation in a fantasy.

As we began exploring the fantasy, Casey revealed that she had always felt judged by her bisexual wife, who always maintained that something was wrong with Casey's sexual development because she had never been with a man. Casey felt ashamed. Perhaps her sexuality was limited or stunted? We wondered together if hurt or anger was contained in the fantasy. Instead of a fantasy that was sexually loving, the gang of men represented her partner's criticisms and shaming. Her partner's words became the violating men, hurting her sexually. But what about her enjoyment in the fantasy?

Casey played with the idea that she would be most aroused if she allowed herself to imagine being one of the men in the fantasy. This was hard for her to accept, being the rapist, but I helped her to work with the fantasy without judgment by suggesting she imagine she was watching a movie. I reminded her that it was just that – a fantasy and not real life. Eventually she had the insight that the fantasy was an enactment of a wish to be more sexually aggressive with her wife, to be able to give her wife the sexual enjoyment that she imagined her wife only experienced with men.

In reality Casey and her wife were experiencing a discrepant desire issue. Casey's wife wished that Casey was more aggressive sexually. The fantasy embodied these conflicts, the shame, humiliation, and anger. Casey not only experienced anger toward her wife but also attempted mastery over it by becoming the male aggressor. She wished, on an unconscious level, that she could be as sexually aggressive as a man. We explored how this fantasy contained a limiting narrative that only men can be sexually aggressive while appreciating the need to distinguish between anger and consensual sexual aggression.

Although initially disturbed by the "queerness/queasiness" of the fantasy, Casey eventually became comfortable using the fantasy while masturbating, and it became part of her repertoire. It had become a normalized part of her sexual experience. She gradually included more men into her fantasies, allowing herself to be a male top at times and other times enjoying the reverse.

Ultimately, she was able to discuss her hurt and anger with her wife. They entered couple sex therapy to heal those issues as well as explore Casey's concerns and conflicts about integrating aggression into sex with her wife. By analyzing what was initially a disturbing fantasy, Casey became comfortable with aggression in sex, reduced her shame about never having been with a man, and embraced and enjoyed playing with masculinity and femininity in her sexuality.

The Case of Jim and Annie: Queer Generational Differences

Harold serves as an example of someone at mid-life whose experience of queerness during sex was confusing and disturbing, so much so that he withdrew from partnered sex to avoid the disturbance. As a man in his fifties, he didn't have the cultural experience that younger people have today, where sex and gender variability is more visible and common.

Today, young adults often use language that expresses expansive sex/gender experiences, such as "bi-curious" (exploring same- and other-sex feelings), L.U.G. (lesbian until graduation), or "genderqueer," re-appropriating words such as "queer" to emphasize the non-binary nature of gender. NRST employs an expansive exploration of the diversity and fluidity of sex/gender experience.

Jim and Annie, a couple in their twenties, represent a different generation than Harold, having been brought up with a wider understanding of sexual behavior. They entered therapy to understand why sex was difficult during most of their four-year relationship. They met in a Queer Studies class in college, becoming friends, political activists, and then lovers. After college they moved to New York and got married. They felt compatible intellectually, politically, emotionally, and spiritually. They were very much in love and wanted to start a family.

A few minutes into their first session, I experienced an amusing queer moment as they introduced themselves as Kinsey scores. Annie said she was a "Kinsey 4" and Jim said he was a "Kinsey 5" (on a scale where 0 represents heterosexual and 6 represents homosexual).

They proceeded, without any prompting by me, to expand on what they said by clarifying that those scores pertained only to their sexual behavior. They were sexually attracted to men and women equally, and fantasized about both when masturbating. Annie had fallen in love with most of the men and women she dated. Jim had only been in love with men before he met Annie. Describing themselves as a "queer couple," they lived and discussed their sexual complexity in a matter-of-fact way.

Expanding Models of Sexual Behavior

When the Kinsey studies on male and female sexuality were published in 1948 and 1953, respectively, a definitional crisis occurred. Prior to Kinsey, public and scientific communities considered same-sex activity an uncommon behavior engaged in by psychologically or morally limited individuals. Sexual behavior placed a person in one of two categories, heterosexual or homosexual, which were believed to be immutable essences of an individual. Even though Freud (1905) presented the idea of inherent bisexuality decades earlier, it hardly took hold in the public imagination until Kinsey and his associates provided empirical evidence for a sexual orientation continuum.

The Kinsey Heterosexuality-Homosexuality Scale (KHHS) was created to describe sexual orientation on a 7-point continuum (0 = exclusively heterosexual through 6 = exclusively homosexual) based on reports of sexual behavior and sexual attraction in Kinsey's subjects (see Figure 6.1).

Kinsey documented a significant incidence of homosexual behavior and responsiveness in males and females. Many combined responses fell in the "bisexual" middle of the continuum. Kinsey argued that humans, like other animals, have the capacity for same- and other-sex involvement, which may

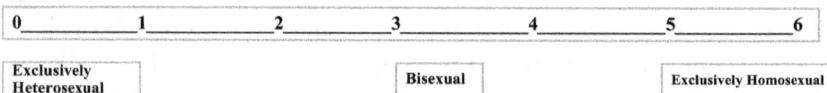

0	1	2	3	4	5	6

Exclusively Heterosexual   Bisexual   Exclusively Homosexual

Figure 6.1

be actualized to different degrees, behaviorally or affectively, at different times over the lifespan. As Kinsey, Pomeroy, and Martin (1948) stated:

> The world is not to be divided into sheep and goats. Not all things are black nor all things white. It is a fundamental of taxonomy that nature rarely deals with discrete categories. Only the human mind invents categories and tries to force facts into separated pigeon-holes. The living world is a continuum in each and every one of its aspects. The sooner we learn this concerning human sexual behavior, the sooner we shall reach a sound understanding of the realities of sex.
>
> (p. 439)

Despite its profound impact, subsequent researchers identified limitations with Kinsey's continuum, most notably that he only studied two aspects of sexual orientation, sexual behavior and sexual attraction, which he assumed were congruent within the individual. Later models, like the Klein Sexual Orientation Grid (KSOG), contain other aspects in addition to behavior and attraction that represent our understanding of the greater complexity of sexual orientation.

The KSOG was developed to extend Kinsey's work by conceptualizing sexual orientation as a multi-variable dynamic process. In addition to sexual behavior and sexual attraction, Klein and his associates (1985) defined five other aspects: sexual fantasy, emotional preference, social preference, sexual self-identification, and heterosexual/homosexual lifestyle preference, making for seven aspects in all (see Figure 6.2).

Individuals rate their experiences on a seven-point continuum. Additionally, the KSOG measures these aspects in relation to the past ("your life since age twenty"), the present ("your life within the past twelve months"),

Based on seven aspects: Sexual behavior, attraction, fantasy, emotional preference, social preference, lifestyle preference and sexual self-identification

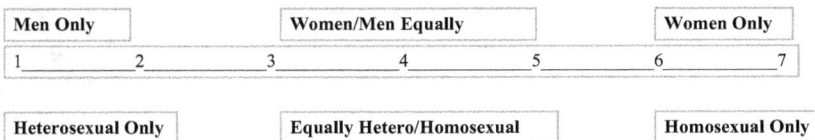

Men Only	Women/Men Equally	Women Only

1	2	3	4	5	6	7

Heterosexual Only	Equally Hetero/Homosexual	Homosexual Only

Figure 6.2

and the ideal ("where you would like to be on the continua"), providing an assessment of the changeability of sexual orientation over the lifespan.

The KSOG may be used to help clients explore the complexity and fluidity of sexual orientation. It is particularly helpful with couples who feel unsettled by variability in sexual orientation in either or both partners. Besides providing clarity about an individual's sexual orientation, it normalizes the incongruence and changeability of same- and other-sex eroticism without forcing a particular meaning onto any given behavior, feeling, or fantasy. It avoids the foreclosure of self-identification and supports the position of not claiming a set identity at all. When utilized in psychotherapy, clients learn to explore dreams, fantasies, wishes, and feelings in an open and curious way. Further expansion of sexual orientation needs to be incorporated into future models to include non-binary, genderqueer, and kink sexual preferences.

A continuum conceptual approach is useful when appreciating diversity in gender identity, experience, and expression, one that deconstructs gender binaries. Arlene Lev (2004) offers a model of sexual identity consisting of four components: sex (male-female), gender (man-woman), sex role (masculine-feminine), and sexual orientation (heterosexual-homosexual) that are flexible, exist on continua, and help us better understand gender-variant behavior and experience (see Figure 6.3).

It represents a shift from a binary system consisting of two sexes that are opposite and different from one another, to one where sex and gender are potentially fluid.

Lev's model doesn't only normalize transgenderism and transsexuality, but also provides an expanded sex/gender approach for all people. Within

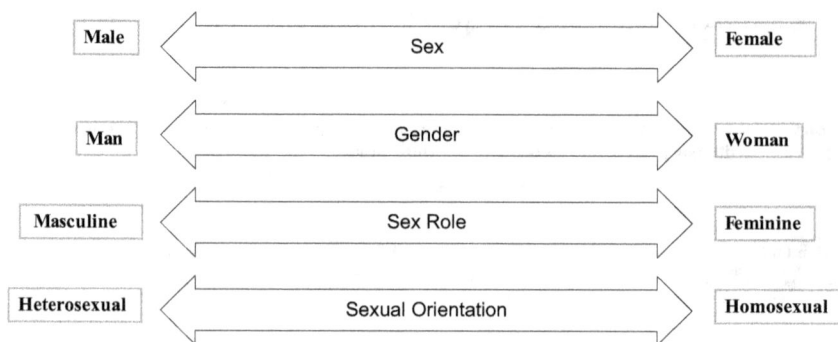

Male	⟷ Sex	Female
Man	⟷ Gender	Woman
Masculine	⟷ Sex Role	Feminine
Heterosexual	⟷ Sexual Orientation	Homosexual

Figure 6.3

this expanded space, one is safe to explore and play; what might have been shamefully repressed becomes available for integration. For example, as in the case of Harold, a heterosexual man may describe his female experience when his wife licks his nipples, or a bisexual woman may express her wish to experience her masculine power by penetrating her husband during anal sex. What a gift we give our clients when they can feel free to investigate whatever sex/gender erotic combinations emerge across these continua.

Exploring the Fluidity and Diversity of Sex Through NRST

The therapeutic goal for Annie and Jim – a queer couple – was to understand why sex was difficult for them from the beginning. They kissed, touched, and performed oral sex and vaginal intercourse. They described sex as awkward, sometimes consisting of power struggles over who controlled what happened. Jim was upset that Annie didn't orgasm with intercourse. It wasn't an issue for her. Annie claimed she embraced a pleasure-based rather than orgasm-based model of sexual response. Jim was performance-based and feared that the reason Annie didn't orgasm was because she wasn't really turned on by him. Since Annie was the first woman with whom he had a committed relationship, Jim harbored insecurities about his ability to sustain the interest of a woman. His waning desire stemmed from his insecurity and disappointment that they didn't both achieve orgasm during intercourse.

I told them that given their gender/sexual fluidity and openness, I was surprised to hear about their conventional sexual menu. They were intrigued and wondered aloud about why they had restricted their items. Were they playing out some unconscious vestiges of internalized heterosexism? Were they unwittingly re-enacting gendered power dynamics internalized from their parents' relationships? They wondered whether their problem was due to their sexual orientations (i.e., perhaps they should be with members of the same sex again). I told them there might be other hypotheses, too, but that I'd first need to conduct in-depth sexual histories.

Annie grew up as the only girl, the youngest child of three, in a traditional Midwestern family. She described how it was difficult to get a word in edgewise or to feel she had much power in the family. She loved her mother, but she remembered from an early age how she hated the devoted wife role her mother lived. "Too much deference to Dad and service to others, at great sacrifice for mom's development," she asserted.

Annie took great pride in her acceptance to an Ivy League school on a full scholarship. In college she embraced her bisexuality and experienced her relationships with women as evidence of her autonomy and independence from all the males women had to contend with on unequal terms.

She told me: "I didn't realize until now that falling in love with and committing to Jim contained old fears about submission from my childhood days."

Jim grew up in a Southern Baptist family of ministers. "My parents were as much married to the church as they were to each other." Jim saw little romance or affection between his parents.

"It seemed to me that my father lacked confidence with my mother," Jim speculated. "She seemed bored with him, but his commitment to the church was an excuse for his inadequate attention to the marriage."

Jim yearned for his father's attention and told me poignant stories of how he'd stay up late at night, waiting to tell his father about his day at school, only to have his father pat him on the head as he walked to his bedroom to change clothes.

"I can't tell you how sad I felt that my father ignored me," Jim said, close to tears. "And what made it worse is how he was different with my two brothers, with whom he played ball and talked sports, which weren't my interests. Looking back, I think he didn't know what to do with a sissy boy."

I said to him: "You sound like you were one of those boys described by the psychoanalyst Richard Isay (1994), whose fathers distance themselves from their gay sons because of their homophobia. It's the reverse of what psychologists used to claim, that distant fathers caused homosexuality."

"I agree with Isay," Jim asserted. "Between my father's religious dogma and his own sexuality – whatever it was – he stayed away from this gay son my whole childhood."

Through the sexual history process, Annie and Jim discovered that their sexual practices with same-sex partners had been an attempt to heal the damage of the messages they received in childhood about sex and gender roles. Annie preferred being the top during strap-on sex with her female partners. She enjoyed the power and the pleasure, often reaching orgasm while observing her partner's excitement.

Jim's favorite sexual activity with men was receptive anal sex, a role he experienced as very active. He loved seducing and being taken. His excitement peaked as he saw his partner's growing desire to "do" him. He loved the orgasms he and his lovers enjoyed together.

In our couple session following the sexual histories, I offered the following summary:

> "Seems like your experience of power during sex with women, Annie, felt like a victory over your oppressive childhood. And for you, Jim, the seduction and being taken process with men represented the desirability and lovability you never felt with your father. Both of you created sexual narratives that helped transform painful childhood feelings."

I went on: "It seems you both associate the healing power of these narratives with a particularly gendered partner. I wonder if we can play with the possibility that the experiences can transcend or blend gendered bodies and meanings, so you may experience the power and pleasures you desire."

"We can have 'genderqueer' sex!" exclaimed Annie, smiling at Jim.

"That's right up our alley," he replied.

I took this opening as an opportunity to suggest some behavioral experimentation.

"How willing would you both be to add strap-on anal sex to your menu? You can take your time and be prepared to discuss how it goes in our next session. Be open to whatever thoughts, feelings, or sensations that arise while you're doing it. There are no rights or wrongs. Anything you experience will provide helpful information."

Annie and Jim were not only willing but were amused that it never occurred to them to expand their sex life in this way. As they expanded their sexual repertoire in the following weeks and months, they were relieved to find greater ease and pleasure than they thought possible. Even though they had queer identities, it didn't occur to them to have queer sex.

As the case histories in this chapter illustrate, helping clients expand their understanding and acceptance of the diversity and fluidity of sexuality, whatever their sexual or gender identifications, will help them discover and embrace their unique sexual complexities so they can have fulfilling sex lives.

CHAPTER 7

✸

WHEN THREE OR MORE IS NOT A CROWD

Non-Monogamy and Polyamory

The practice of consensual non-monogamy (CNM) and polyamory are not for the faint of heart. They are expansive relational practices that, if done well, require a commitment to high levels of consciousness, communication, and emotional intelligence. Although there are more lay books written about both, the therapeutic community lags far behind, living in a vacuum devoid of affirmative theoretical frames and technique. NRST can begin to fill that vacuum.

Polyamory involves having multiple emotional/sexual relationships, one of which may include a marriage or primary relationship. It's a relationship practice that assumes it is possible (and acceptable) to love many people and to maintain multiple intimate and sexual relationships. Polyamory provides the excitement of a new love with the security of a stable base. When it works, it can produce the perfect brain chemistry blend: simultaneous access to both the attraction and attachment phases of romantic love.

Cultures around the world have different forms/names for it – polygamy, polyandry, and polyfidelity are a few. Polyfidelity means that people are sexually exclusive among members of a whole group, almost like monogamy for an entire group of people.

Polyamory has its roots in the Kerista community formed in New York City during the 1950s. An extended community later developed in the Haight-Ashbury section of San Francisco in the 1970s. In the '60s and '70s, the sexual revolution was gaining popularity, and open relationships became more common in general society.

In my practice I'm seeing more and more people who are in open relationships or who are interested in forming one than I did twenty years ago.

During the AIDS crisis of the 1980s, attitudes toward open relationships shifted. The sexual freedom of the '60s and '70s seemed dangerous at a time when unprotected sex was risky, even life threatening.

People were much more focused on forming monogamous relationships. Now, many years later, with medications that make people safer as it relates to HIV, open relationships are becoming more prevalent again.

Another factor is that the internet has totally changed the sexual landscape. Today, an anonymous partner can be instantaneously had with a touch of an iPhone. Because of the ease of connecting with someone, open relationships are no longer a niche type of thing, or just an urban thing, or a phenomenon that the heterosexual community "caught" from the gay community. Today, total strangers can create open relationship arrangements or develop polyamorous relationships pretty quickly, and also find an accepting community of like-minded people.

Many people give credit to the gay male community for normalizing consensual non-monogamy and open relationships. The gay male community historically has taken great pride in not assuming that the enduring bond in male couples had to do with sex. For many gay men, committing to someone or marrying them is an emotional rather than a sexual commitment.

I'm seeing more gay men, perhaps because of marriage equality, who are monogamous and don't want to open their relationship. Other couples practice "don't ask, don't tell," or are what sex columnist Dan Savage calls "monogamish" (Oppenheimer, 2011). These couples open the relationship now and then, or under certain circumstances, like only having threesomes. And some still develop fully open relationships.

Sex at Dawn, a controversial book by evolutionary scientists Christopher Ryan and Cacilda Jethá (2011), make a strong argument for the unnaturalness of monogamy. The authors document that monogamy is not a natural thing and never was, but rather was an outgrowth of capitalism and property ownership. Especially in heterosexual relationships, the wife was viewed as the property of the man. But left to our own devices, none of us would be monogamous.

More people today are questioning monogamy. With marriage now an option for gay people, perhaps we're seeing "the queering of marriage." Marriage has made LGBT people more traditional, but LGBT people have also affected and questioned the assumptions of traditional marriage. Now, more children have two mommies, two daddies, or non-binary parents. In LGBT relationships and families, traditional arrangements and roles are disrupted. Why not monogamy, too?

Why Couples Discuss Open Relationship in Therapy

Some couples are interested in exploring whether they can have a partner on the side, and they need help in deciding whether and how to do that and, equally important, why they want to do it. Some people believe opening a relationship will help revive a stagnant primary relationship or help them manage differences in sexual interests. Some people enter therapy already in open relationship and are doing fine, but they need to decide how to tell children, family, or friends about it. Others in an open relationship are having trouble managing jealousy, envy, or competition.

Some couples consider an open relationship after one of them has had an affair and first need to work out the betrayal issues. Such a crisis can prompt a couple to the realization that monogamy hasn't worked for one or both of them. Therapy can be challenging if one wants open relationship and the other doesn't.

Polyamory versus polysexuality (sex with no strings attached) is more psychologically "labor intensive," because each partner added into the "family system" introduces more emotional, sexual, and family complexity to understand and manage. Remember when I said earlier that "all sex is group sex?" Well, in cases of polyamory, group dynamics expand exponentially. Why, then, would someone want to engage in such a relationship arrangement? It can, under the right circumstances, be sexually, emotionally and socially transformative.

Before clients make a decision to open up a relationship for more sexual and/or emotional connection, I explain to them what open relationships are and how to use the NRST process, to clarify whether it's a good option and what they can expect from it.

Exploring Narratives About Open Relationships

I first explore with clients the many untrue narratives about open relationships. Some clients believe that people who want open relationships are immature, commitment phobic, or selfishly want to have it all, both the security of a marriage and the freedom of single life. Some therapists who believe this as well say to clients, "Choose your option, kiddo. You can't have your cake and eat it, too!"

When I lecture on this topic, many therapists say to me, "Suzanne, tell the truth. Open relationships don't work. Isn't it really an exit ramp toward a divorce or breakup?" They doubt there's any track record for success in open relationships.

This may be true for some people, but it certainly isn't true for everyone, based on my many years of working with clients. In reality, I've had only a few couples who have broken up after trying an open relationship. It may be because of the careful assessment I conduct of their sexual histories and family relations through the NRST process in couple therapy.

Couples who succeed in an open relationship are willing to work at it — and it requires a lot of work. I often say to clients, "You don't have a good body as you get older because of luck. You have a good body because you watch what you eat, go to the gym, and do all those sit-ups and pull-ups. An open relationship requires the same commitment." If opening up is not for the purpose of transforming a primary relationship into a friendship, clients have to work diligently and consciously to protect the primary relationship. It requires mastering feelings of jealousy, envy, and competition, as well as understanding childhood attachment experiences, wounds, and narratives.

Three Major Reasons

People generally explore open relationships for three major reasons.

The first is the loss of desire in long-term relationships. Both partners often lack any sense of how to address this issue. They have real doubt about whether their desire will ever come back. They don't know that loss of desire is normal. They don't know that sex can begin with willingness, not desire. They don't know that desire could follow arousal or even orgasm, so they consider opening the relationship.

The second reason is sexual incompatibility. One partner may have lost interest in sex. It's completely off their radar screen, and they have no desire to revive it. The challenge is that they are partnered with someone who has an average or even highly charged libido who wants to have sex in their life.

Some people have little or no interest in partnered sex, because they are asexual. It's their sexual orientation. Before people knew about the possibility of asexuality, one person who's not asexual could marry someone who is, without even knowing that such a thing exists. This may only surface years later in their relationship, and may become known only with the help of a therapist. In such a case one person could agree to a no-sex marriage, the other person could push themself to be sexual, they could end the relationship, or open it.

Or perhaps there are discrepant sexual preferences, where one partner, for example, is into BDSM as their favorite thing to do, but they're living with a committed vanilla person, who prefers conventional, non-kinky sex.

Even if the vanilla partner was willing to try some BDSM play, it may not cut it.

The third reason, which is less common but emerging more with younger people, is a belief that the institution of monogamous marriage is antiquated and unhealthy, based on patriarchy or rooted in capitalistic society. This is more of a philosophical or political stance.

The most common challenge leading to an open marriage remains the loss of desire. This often happens in a "peer" relationship, which we discussed in Chapter 1, where two people are best friends, have a great deal of trust, and where the relationship means a lot to them. They have a long and companionate history together. Perhaps they are raising kids. They don't have a strong sexual connection with one another, but the relationship as a whole means a lot more to them than breaking up to have a more fulfilling sexual life.

For many couples, there has to be an alternative to either a sexless marriage or one where there's disparate desire or too many differences in sexual preference. Opening the relationship can become a viable option for those who can learn to navigate it well.

I tend to reserve suggesting opening up as an option until later in therapy, especially if the couple isn't on the verge of breaking up. My first approach, as always, is to uncover and examine those unconscious narratives connected to lack of desire or incompatibility. If a couple is not in an immediate crisis situation, I conduct the relational sexual histories to see if there's enough capability to revive or sustain the relationship. I explain the human sexual response cycle and introduce them to the concept of willingness.

I won't raise the option of opening up until the couple has spent quite a lot of time in therapy, nothing much has changed, and the couple doesn't want to break up. Then I might say, "Since you want to stay together but are still having these problems, have you ever thought of opening the relationship or having some kind of consensual non-monogamy agreement?" Some couples reject that option out of hand while others are willing to explore it.

Can It Work?

An open relationship is not something that can be done in a casual way. Whether the arrangement will actually improve a relationship is a complicated question. In general, couples who have a poor or non-existent sex life and who approach an open relationship to spice up their sex life are on tenuous ground unless they understand why their sex life is suboptimal in the first place.

Couples who have the best results with open relationship are those whose primary relationship with one another is emotionally and sexually strong to begin with, but who are opening up the relationship because they want variety, or who feel fine about outsourcing all or some sexual parts of their relationship.

It's rare that each partner in an open relationship has the same experience of it. That, in itself, can create trouble. I often have to help couples manage a situation where one of them is having frequent, great sex and the other partner is feeling frustrated and deprived. Or, one partner prefers polyamory, sometimes increasing jealousy and competition in the other partner. The NRST process helps clients assess, anticipate, and manage an open relationship in a way that doesn't create more problems than the couple originally had.

Conducting a Thorough Relational Sexual History Assessment

Using the relational sexual history process, I conduct an extensive assessment of how differentiated the partners are and their ability to tolerate their partner having a new relationship. The more merged a couple is, the more they believe they have to have the same feelings and experiences, the less of a chance that an open relationship will work. Couples do better if they can allow for two different subjectivities and sets of needs. Such couples are able to live with difference and manage the details well.

I create a genogram (like a family tree) and look at their family histories with them. I have them predict their ability to tolerate jealousy, envy, competition, and feelings of betrayal given their family and relationship histories. We take a look at their family systems. For example, what kind of relationship did their parents have? Trustworthy or not? Were there secrets or betrayals? What kind of relationship did they have with their siblings? Did they compete a lot with a brother or sister? Was there an Oedipal victory, i.e., did they "win" one of their parent's affections over the other? What feelings were involved? What were the consequences? Were they winners or losers in family competition for love or affection? Did they get the attention they needed or not?

After taking their histories and assessing them with the couple, they may decide not to pursue an open relationship because of its potential pitfalls. Or, aware of the pitfalls, they may be better able to manage an open relationship if they pursue one. I make the decision-making process complicated because, in the long run, that kind of preparation will give them the patience, consciousness, knowledge, and communication tools to success-fully manage the relationship when things get tough.

The people who do best in open relationships are people who 1) are com-mitted to the growth of self, partner, and the relationship; 2) have good communication skills and a high degree of emotional differentiation, i.e., they are fully able to allow their partner to have a different subjectivity; and 3) experience the partner's privacy as non-threatening.

These qualities form the basis of any strong relationship. There is a lot of respect, a lot of support, and a lot of equality. Partners are committed to good teamwork, figuring out what works best for both people.

Establishing Clear Guidelines

If a couple decides to open the relationship, it's best to establish clear guide-lines before doing so (Nelson, 2013; Taormino, 2008). For example, will they have sex with someone the other partner knows? Or should they only have sex with strangers? Can they have sex with a new partner in their home? Or is that off limits? Are they going to practice safer sex? How do they prevent themselves from falling in love if they simply want sex and not an emotional connection? Some couples are swinging couples and would never allow the other partner to be alone with someone else. Instead, sex only happens in a threesome.

It's important to make guidelines that allow for slips by encouraging transparency, trust, and honesty. Some long-time practitioners of open rela-tionship assert that the most important positive quality of the arrangement is not all the good sex but the amount of trust, good communication, and honesty in the primary relationship.

It helps to enter a set of guidelines allowing for error. The couple can have an agreement that allows the erring partner to be transparent and open about what went wrong. For example, a couple may have established guidelines about safer sex. They allow their partner to have penetration with someone outside the relationship, but they must always use a condom. But what happens if he drinks too much, loses himself in the heat of the moment, and doesn't use a condom? Instead of slamming that erring partner, which can lead to shame and keeping secrets, partners can create an atmosphere where they can talk about what can be done to prevent a recurrence. If there's a drug or alcohol issue, it can be discussed and examined. Perhaps the agreement has to be reworked to prevent a future slip – no drinking or drugs on sex dates.

In addition to building trust, this also offers the opportunity to analyze and revise the original agreement. Perhaps it was a little bit too restrictive. It can be changed to address complications or newly discovered desires that made it hard to keep the agreement.

Avoidance or Mastery?

Many therapists have a negative view of open relationships because they think people use them to avoid dealing with unresolved emotional issues. Let's say a woman's father left her during childhood. If she pursues an open relationship, the negative view is that she wants both a husband and a boyfriend because her father left her and she needs a sense of protection to compensate for that. Or she's commitment phobic because her father abandoned her. She needs a backup plan; she can't put all her eggs in one basket. By opening the relationship, she's replicating negative patterns instead of engaging in personal growth.

But there's another view, which I fully embrace — the alternative idea that people can master attachment wounds or challenges through an open relationship.

Let's say a man had a mother who was very intrusive, almost emotionally incestuous. Not sexually or physically abusive, but inappropriate emotionally. His father didn't protect him and he couldn't stand up to his mother. He never learned how to set up or maintain healthy boundaries. He didn't feel entitled to have them.

As he engages in an open relationship and finds a boyfriend, he can learn the skills of navigating what he wants. When both his husband and boyfriend want him on the same night, he's able to say, "Sorry, this is what I want," and tolerate disappointing the other person. This could provide a way for him to master the earlier attachment difficulty.

Mastery may operate also in relation to kink, which I'll discuss more fully in Chapter 8. For example, if someone was physically abused in childhood and now has a spanking fetish, some therapists will say, "Oh my God, she's just a masochist. She's just repeating the same pain she suffered with her father."

That's certainly possible, but it's also possible that she's mastering that past trauma. She's the one who's calling the shots. She's choosing the guy. She's choosing what gets done and when. She has her safe word; she can say no. So it could be an empowering experience for this woman to be spanked, whereas in childhood she was being abused.

Viewing Open Relationships Through the Framework of Family Systems Therapy

My theoretical framework for open relationships and their possibility for mastery comes from the family therapy field, where systems containing more than two people are commonly described, examined, and understood. From a family therapy perspective, when a couple decides to open a relationship, especially if it's going to include long-term relationships and not just one-night stands, it's like having children. The couple already has a family tree (called the genogram in family therapy) and now they're adding members to it, just as if a child has been born.

This is especially true in polyamorous situations, where a new love interest could be part of a family system for years. Some people wind up living together as a triad, a committed couple living with someone's boyfriend or girlfriend. Some triads have kids and raise them together. Some therapists view this as a radically different family unit from the Ozzie and Harriet days, and culturally it may be, but dynamically it's still a family system.

The main theoretical framework that I believe helps therapists understand and address the complexities and challenges of an open relationship is from family therapy. A major thinker I rely on in the field is the American psychiatrist Murray Bowen, one of the founders of Systemic Family Therapy, who viewed the family (versus the individual) as an emotional unit. When clients enter therapy, problems are viewed as a function of the family system.

One of Bowen's (Kerr & Bowen, 1988) major contributions was the concept of differentiation, the ability to be in emotional contact yet autonomous in one's own emotional functioning. In his view, if parents were poorly differentiated, meaning they were merged and couldn't allow each other to have a separate opinion, the child of those parents could only reach the same level of differentiation. The child's level of differentiation was pretty much fixed, almost like a genetic inheritance. Today we know that's not totally true, that there are ways you can work with people to help develop their level of differentiation. People are not prisoners of their family history.

Bowen studied the movement from the dyad of the married couple to the triangle when adding a child. Unlike Freud who viewed the Oedipal triangle as the root of neuroses, fraught with conflict and competition, Bowen normalized the triangle as potentially having a stabilizing effect on the dyad, depending on the level of differentiation in the system. For Freud, triangles were problematic. They involved acting out, reenacting childhood wounds, splitting, and avoiding conflict.

For Bowen, triangles are an inevitable part of any family's emotional system; they have the potential to be healthy or unhealthy. When you open a relationship, the new triangle can be a formula for disaster, creating an Oedipal drama. Bowen's work on family systems allows for this unhealthy possibility. On the other hand, Bowen discussed the ways that a triangle can be psychologically healthy. Bowen talked about an "overlay of differentiation." The more differentiated people are, the more they are able to tolerate fluidity in their relationships to one another. They have the ability to tolerate the fluidity of the Oedipal triangle. Sometimes it might be equilateral, with the sides equal; at other times it might be isosceles, with the sides unequal, but these changes don't have to create emotional distress.

When therapists apply Bowenian theory to open relationship, it's a valid and more expansive way of thinking about why some couples do well and some don't.

For example, consider a situation where a wife has a boyfriend, and all three of them (wife, husband, and boyfriend) are friends. They're comfortable with one another and even socialize together. But one night after having dinner together, the wife decides to go home with the boyfriend instead of the husband. The equilateral triangle they had now shifts into an isosceles, because the husband has to go home alone. If the couple is well-differentiated, has good communication skills, and a solid emotional foundation, they can face such a situation with flexibility and empathy. If poorly differentiated, the change in triangular relationship can create conflict.

Compersion: The Practice of Unconditional Empathy

Compersion is the ability to be happy rather than jealous about a partner having a good sexual/emotional experience with another person. There's great pride in the poly community in being able to transform jealousy into compersion, to be happy about a partner's happiness.

If a couple is well-differentiated, the husband can practice compersion when his wife goes home with her boyfriend. He could say, "I'm really happy my wife is going to have a good time with John tonight. I'm either going to pick up some woman on the way home, or I'm going to go home alone and just say, 'I really hope my wife has a good time.'" A husband who is not well-differentiated could start a fight with John or call his wife at midnight and demand she come home. In this case, the couple needs to explore why the husband became so dysregulated. Is it in reaction to something happening in the present relationship, or a trigger from his family history, or both?

Attachment theory and family therapy help people develop a language for the various levels of relating clients want to achieve. When relational triangles shift from equilateral to isosceles, clients strive to be flexible, relying on transparency, trust, and good communication. Pre-planning a process is helpful. If the wife is hoping to be with the boyfriend more often, the husband and the wife can have some couple sessions to talk about how that would work best for each partner (sometimes sessions may include a poly partner as well).

In a couple session the husband might say, "Why don't you be with your boyfriend on Tuesday nights, because that's when I get home late after big meetings at work. If you were home with me on Tuesday night, we couldn't really enjoy each other that much anyway." And the wife might agree. In this case they are working as a team where each person's needs get identified, discussed, and accommodated as much as possible. That's what makes families of all kinds work well.

Mastering the Oedipal Triangle Through Polyamory

If someone was an Oedipal victor in childhood, they can now, in a poly triangle, learn how to enjoy being in the chosen position and not feel like they're hurting the other person – like they felt about the excluded parent in their childhood. They no longer have to avoid being the chosen one because of the anxiety or guilt they felt as a child. They can be more fluid as triangles change and can actually master the Oedipal triangle feelings/wounds from childhood.

Some people in poly relationships experience little jealousy. When I do some exploration, I usually find such a person was well-nurtured as a child, perhaps had the gleam in the caregiver's eye. They unconsciously carry positive narratives about themselves from childhood into the poly experience later on. They may feel little jealousy about their partner's girlfriend or boyfriend because they have a secure feeling that they are desirable and valued.

In contrast, a child who grows up with a sense of jealousy, competition, and envy because their mother favored a sibling, or who experienced no gleam in the eye of any caregiver, may be especially triggered by a poly situation. For it to work, they have to become aware of their early childhood experiences and feelings in therapy. This is another example of how early childhood experiences can influence one's ability to bring flexibility to adult sexual relationships.

The potential to work through early attachment wounds is profound, partly because an open relationship has the potential to intensely expose those wounds. But by exposing them and confronting them, rather than avoiding them, they can also be healed.

The Case of John and Mary: Using an Open Relationship to Master Childhood Wounds

One example of mastering childhood wounds through an open relationship involves the case of John and Mary. When they came to see me, Mary complained about John's performance in bed and said they rarely had sex. Through John's sexual history we found out he had an intrusive mother who made him feel very unsafe about sex and sexual boundaries; he brought these issues into the marriage and projected them onto Mary. It wasn't that he married his mother, because Mary was not the intrusive type. But due to John's history, almost anything she would say – even something as seemingly innocuous as "Could you put the milk back in the refrigerator?" – was experienced as controlling and intrusive. So John made Mary into his mother, which diminished his sexual desire and comfort.

In her frustration, Mary suggested to John that he go to a party with her friends, who were part of the local poly community. John was surprised how erotically charged he felt at the parties, as was Mary. He kissed women at some parties, and she kissed both men and women. Within this safe sex-positive community, they were able to allow themselves a little sexual pleasure as long as they were together.

In looking at this experience more deeply, John began to realize that he felt safer and more confident sexually with more than one person in the room, and especially with Mary there.

"In a funny way," said John, "Mary changed from my sexually threatening mother to my sexually supportive ally." Mary was relieved to hear about the role change.

As we talked about it, they decided to enter into an open relationship. They wanted the safety of being with each other, while allowing themselves to play with different arrangements of people. John began to experience his sexuality with more than one person; this was easier for him than the dyadic relationship with Mary, which had led to his sexual shutdown.

John's sexual boundaries began to be threatened when women asked for various sexual practices and he couldn't say no. Through his wife and friends in the poly community, he learned to set boundaries. He learned how to become aware of his needs and choose what he wanted and didn't want sexually in a way he was never able to do in his marriage. The power of the transference from his mother to his wife regressed John, but within the poly community he was able to find his adult voice and sexual agency.

Open relationship provided Mary with her own mastery as well. She experienced a dreadfully long loss of her mother, who died from cancer when Mary was eleven years old. After her mother died, she and her three brothers were left to fend for themselves as her father disappeared into his work life. Mary yearned for the mother she remembered, who was kind and attentive, and her father, who was playful and fun before illness struck. Mary remembered how affectionate and excited her parents were when they dressed up to go on date nights every Saturday. Her parents gave her the sense that sexuality in a loving relationship was a good thing.

"I lost my mother at such a crucial time right before I got my period and started becoming a woman," Mary shared sadly. "And my father escaped the loss through his work. So, I never had a sense of my worth as a loving or sexual person from then on."

When she met and married John, Mary felt like life was giving her a second chance at happiness. They had such a good sexual and emotional life in the beginning, until John started experiencing everything Mary did as an intrusion. Having had the early loss of her mother and father made it that much harder for Mary when John started sexually and emotionally withdrawing from her. She felt abandoned all over again.

When John started to become sexually alive again in the poly community, Mary felt hope for the first time that they might be able to re-connect sexually and emotionally. She was surprised to find their group sexual experiences as more enjoyable than threatening. A crucial element was John's great need and appreciation for her help to find his sexual voice, and the experience of such a loving poly community that felt like she regained the happy family that she lost when her mother died. The icing on the cake was John's renewed sexual interest in Mary as her role as intrusive mother shifted back to sexual partner. As she regained John and gained a new community family, she was able to more deeply grieve all she lost in childhood as a result of her mother's illness and death.

As John and Mary engaged more fully with the poly community, I helped them create a contract of what they needed from their relationship when they eventually wanted to pursue sexual experiences outside of each other's presence. Part of the contract was that they had to approve of each other's partners. They also agreed that they could call a halt to their outside activities if they felt that their primary relationship was being overly stressed or harmed. They found that not only did their emotional and sexual lives improve from their experiences in the poly community, but that open relationship was curative well beyond what they expected.

It's important that couples who want to open their relationship develop a contract to establish ground rules and protect the primary relationship. But it's just as important that partners explore and understand their relational sexual histories, to help identify and predict what childhood factors might make a poly relationship challenging and healing. NRST work involves helping each partner identify what might be re-activated and how to constructively work through it together. Our wounds are tied up with our sexuality, but sexuality can also heal our wounds. Through an open relationship, unconscious wounds can become conscious, the first step in making peace with the past.

Coming Out About Open Relationships and Polyamory

Open relationships and polyamory present a number of coming-out issues.

The biggest issue with poly arrangements isn't coming out to friends who are non-poly or in traditional relationships, but in coming out to children. One partner might say, "I don't want to come out to our kids; it will hurt them deeply," and the other one might say, "We're living a lie if we don't come out. It's a bad message."

These conversations sound similar to those of gay and lesbian couples struggling with coming out decades ago. I'm old enough to remember the days when homophobia was so prevalent that people would leave a heterosexual marriage, connect with a same-sex partner, and still refuse to come out to their children from the marriage. They were now living with a male or female "roommate." They couldn't tell the children or other family members the truth. That used to be a common issue, and for some people it still is. I recently worked with a lesbian couple in their forties who were not comfortable being out with family members. One woman's family didn't know she's in a relationship at all. When they visited the other woman's family, she introduced her partner as her friend or roommate.

Staying in the closet can cause major fights for a couple, even though kids or other family members often assume they are gay. But not too many years ago people were ostracized if they came out. Children could be ridiculed or beaten up at school if they had queer parents. Or the couple might be afraid of their children being ashamed of them or rejecting them, or of losing them in custody fights.

I've heard these same arguments among poly couples who have kids. If one is poly first, then have kids, it's usually easier or more natural to come out than if one is a parent in a monogamous relationship first and then comes out as poly. Parents often discuss how to explain to the kids the change from monogamous to poly and what it means for the primary relationship and family. How does one explain the boyfriend or girlfriend, who a parent wants to spend the holidays with or travel with?

If a poly couple is in agreement about telling their children, they don't usually need therapeutic help. These couples believe in an alternative form of family. They want to normalize polyamory for their children. They have an expansive view of love and family that is enriching, not threatening.

Some couples can't agree on coming out based on philosophical differences, and other times those conflicts can be related to family history. The person who doesn't want to come out may have grown up in a secretive family or in a family where there were negative consequences when a secret was revealed. My role is to help them work through the historical narratives that may be limiting the couple's ability to find a path forward.

Elisabeth Sheff (2015), in her book *The Polyamorists Next Door*, notes that:

> Polyamorous parents came out to their children in a variety of ways, and at a variety of points in their relationships, depending on the age of the children, the past and current familial configurations, and factors external to the family. Sometimes parents come out at different times or in different ways to their various children, tailoring the timing and information to the children's needs and the family situation. If a child is born into a polyamorous family, parents will often wait until the children ask something about the family and then give age- appropriate information in direct response to a request.
>
> (p. 219)

Sheff also notes the benefits to children of having poly parents:

> One of the major advantages poly parents mention is the plentiful positive role modeling available to children in poly families. These role models include ethical considerations like honesty, a willingness to meet

other's needs, and careful communication and negotiation. Perhaps most importantly, parents emphasize the relationships between their children, partners, and friends as sources of personal role modeling through life examples and advice.

(p. 299)

Quite often, therapists will be caught in the middle between partners with opposing points of view. One partner might say to me, "What do you think? Isn't it healthier that the children know we're poly?" And the other will respond, "Oh no, Suzanne, it could be traumatizing or confusing for them, right? They're just learning about their sexuality."

Whether the issue is gayness or open relationships or polyamory, one or both partners may engage the therapist to be the decider. I often say to clients: "I didn't go to law school. I'm not a judge, I'm a psychologist. My job is to hold the space for the differences between you two right now, to help you be curious about them, and to help you find where the compromise might be."

My advice to therapists is to help poly couples find ways to compromise about coming out. They may not fully disclose everything to their children, but perhaps they'll introduce their outside partners to their children or invite them over for holidays. They can slowly begin to integrate their partners into their lives instead of having one big sit-down announcement. In such a compromise, each partner might have to give a little. Look for such a middle ground in working with these clients.

Open Relationship: When Partners Aren't Equally Ready

I want to make the distinction between an open relationship being right for someone versus being ready for an open relationship. Some people come to the understanding that such a relationship will never be right for them, but they are okay with that. It's very difficult when it's right for one person in the couple and the other person is neither ready nor okay with it. In that case, what do they do?

In some cases, the person who isn't ready for it goes ahead anyway, because they're afraid they're going to lose their partner if they don't. That kind of situation often creates many bumps in the road. The partner who isn't comfortable can end up harboring resentment, hurt, and rejection; they experience the opposite of compersion. They're not happy when they know their partner's out playing with someone else. The anger they feel comes back around to the relationship. The other partner could feel a combination of defensiveness, guilt, or resentment about having their right to sexual freedom curtailed.

To help couples who experience this difference in readiness, I have them identify feelings and values by asking a series of questions like:

- What does monogamy mean to them? Non-monogamy?
- How do they describe past relationships that were monogamous/open?
- What fuels feelings of jealousy from their childhood? Now?
- How much do they value transparency versus privacy?
- How well do they know their needs?
- How easy it for them to express their needs?
- What do they need most from each other?
- What helps them feel safe and secure in the relationship?
- How do they compromise when their needs diverge?

A key part of the emotional assessment, as always, is looking at family history. Someone might say, "My father had an affair for years, which totally humiliated my mother. I held her while she was crying. Every time my husband goes out with his girlfriend, it's going to wind up like my father and mother all over again. Can't do it."

Or a gay man who lost friends to AIDS might say, "I can't be in a relationship that's not monogamous, because I just lost too many people who were close to me."

Asking hard questions of both partners will help you determine what the partners need to identify and work through to be right for it or ready for it. It might not be right for one of them, ever, or it could just be that they need more time to feel ready for it. If it's the latter, the therapist's role is to help them work on the issues associated with an open relationship as they would for running a marathon – carefully and thoroughly. NRST can be the foundation for that process.

CHAPTER 8

※

WE'RE ALL A LITTLE BIT KINKY

How do you define kink? It's kind of like defining porn: you know it when you see it, but you can't always give a specific definition. What's vanilla for somebody is kink for another. One person's kink is the next person's vanilla.

But, in general, kink is defined as non-conventional sexual desires, practices, or fantasies. It can involve some of the following: spanking, whipping, urinating, defecating, master/slave sex, vaginal or anal fisting, bondage, nipple clamps, cock and ball play, piercing, slapping, punching, biting, scratching, erotic role-playing, knife play, electricity play, sadomasochism, domination, submission, leather play, and fetishes.

Fetishes, a subset of kink, involve sexual desire focused on inanimate objects (i.e., stockings) or specific body parts (i.e., feet).

The term "vanilla sex" is defined as conventional sex that conforms to basic cultural expectations, consisting of "regular" sexual activities such as intercourse, touching, and kissing.

When therapists are taught about kink, the connotations usually are negative. Many kink practitioners don't go to therapists, unless they know they are kink-friendly, in much the same way that gay people avoided therapy in the past, afraid that therapists would view them pathologically and try to convert them to heterosexuality.

For a long time in the psychological canon, kink activities were classified as perversions, which, in the not-so-distant past, also included homosexuality. It wasn't until 1973 that the American Psychiatric Association removed homosexuality from its *Diagnostic and Statistical Manual of Mental Disorders* (DSM-II). Before then, homosexuality and any kind of bondage or S&M was considered unhealthy. There was nothing deemed healthy about any kink-related sexual activity.

Homosexuality was the first "perversion" that was challenged within the psychological community, creating a shift in thinking that it didn't matter whether one's love object was of the same or opposite sex. In this view, both heterosexual and homosexual relationships could be healthy or unhealthy. A merged gay couple could be as problematic as a merged heterosexual couple. A gay couple could be as sexually dysfunctional as a heterosexual one. Relationship "health" was no longer based on the gender of the partners.

In the 1980s and '90s, a lot of affirmative psychological work about LGB issues emerged, first within academia and then within the psychoanalytic and greater psychotherapy community. A major reason for the wave was the refusal of LGB clinicians to remain closeted as they entered and completed professional training. They essentially began to say to their psychotherapy communities, "we're here, we're queer, we're your students, your teachers, your analysts, your therapists, and your supervisors." This professional coming out created a huge shift from stigma and shame to healthy homosexuality, from "perversion" to "preference." An argument of these professional advocates was that the "real perversion" or sickness associated with homosexuality had to do with homophobia, not homosexuality. Subsequently, assessment of LGB clients included exploring the degree of internalized homophobia that could take the form of commitment avoidance, depression, substance abuse, an inability to come out, or sexual problems.

More recently, trans activism has helped to remove the pathological connotations associated with gender dysphoria, an internal state where someone feels distressed because of a mismatch between their assigned gender and their gender identity. Gender dysphoria is no longer considered to be a "condition" that needs to be analyzed and fixed. Instead of being seen as a perversion, gender dysphoria is now understood as an experience associated with gender incongruity, sometimes leading to hormone and/or surgical remedies and sometimes not.

Additionally, therapists (trans and cis gendered) are becoming aware of the necessity to explore the degree of transphobia TGNC clients might have internalized, helping clients parse out how much of their gender dysphoria is due to societal prejudice, or the secondary trauma associated with continued violence against trans people. For example, the murder rate of transgender women, the majority of whom are women of color, has been increasing in recent years (Holter, 2017).

In the same way over the past decade, some kink activities are no longer seen as shameful and pathological, even entering the mainstream. For example, cross-dressers, once hidden in the shadows, are now part of our pop cultural fabric; think RuPaul, an American drag queen whose Emmy Award–winning television show, *RuPaul's Drag Race*, has been a hit since 2009. Or, the mega-hit book *Fifty Shades of Grey*, which spawned films and a cottage industry of BDSM products. In 2017, Princeton University joined other Ivy League colleges in hosting a BDSM club for students.

Still, many therapists continue to hold misconceptions about kink because working with kink clients can be anxiety-provoking. Some people are into dripping hot wax onto one another; others wear diapers during sex. The central conflict for many therapists is this: are people who engage in kink practices harming themselves or others? If so, what is the therapist's responsibility? Given the lack of informed, non-pathologizing training on kink, therapists often feel at a loss.

First, let's start with identifying common negative narratives about kink. Psychologist Margaret Nichols (2006), who specializes in LGBTQ, kink, and consensual non-monogamy, often discusses misconceptions about kink. Following are some that many therapists have internalized from society and/or professional training experiences:

- BDSM is mostly about the "dominant" exploiting a passive "submissive."
- BDSM is about physical pain.
- BDSM activities inevitably escalate to extremes and/or become addictive.
- BDSM is self-destructive.
- BDSM stems from childhood abuse.
- BDSM is an avoidance of intimacy.
- BDSM is separate from "vanilla" sex.

(pp. 283–5)

Mastery Versus Harm?

Because therapists are bound by ethical and legal responsibilities – "do no harm" is our basic guideline – we have an obligation to break confidentiality if someone is suicidal or planning to harm someone else. For some therapists, kink is viewed as doing harm. Some therapists have a hard time with clients who are sexually aroused by giving or receiving pain. Some people are aroused by being cut or cutting their partner, or burning themselves or others with candle wax. Some men are turned on by having their testicles nailed to a board, a form of CBT (Cock and Ball Torture).

Even a trained sex therapist could feel squeamish about these practices, but feeling squeamish is different from believing an activity is pathological. Even people who practice kink can be turned off by certain sexual acts. (In fact, there's a term for that within the kink community: "squicked" means having a strong negative reaction to an activity without judging it.) It's important that therapists own their countertransference when working with all clients, but especially with kink clients. If a therapist is emotionally triggered by bondage, they need to learn to constructively deal with those feelings, or make a referral to a kink-friendly therapist. The problem in this case is not with the sexual activity but with the therapist's level of discomfort and judgment of the activity.

So, the question remains: where does one draw the line in whether a sexual activity is harmful?

The Case of Vanessa: What Is a Therapist to Think?

Vanessa likes to be paddled or whipped, and she also suffered from childhood abuse. Her father often beat her whenever she defied his wishes. Now, as an adult in therapy, Vanessa reveals that she is into spanking.

For some therapists, Vanessa's sexual preference can't possibly be healthy. How do we know that the client isn't reenacting an old script in a damaging way? Has shameful abuse been merely repackaged as consensual S&M or kink play?

When Madonna's coffee table book, *Sex*, came out in 1992, it flew off the bookshelves. It contained a lot of S&M imagery: Madonna in a dog collar and getting whipped. People questioned how could Madonna, a feminist, let herself be dominated? Wasn't that anti-feminist objectification?

In her acceptance speech for the Billboard Woman of the Year Award, Madonna answered this question, aimed at one of her most vocal critics:

> Camille Paglia, the famous feminist writer, said that I set women back by objectifying myself sexually. Oh, I thought, "so if you're a feminist, you don't have sexuality, you deny it." So I said, "**** it. I'm a different kind of feminist. I'm a bad feminist."
>
> (Kreps, 2016)

When someone is abused in childhood, the child wasn't controlling the show. It was the complete opposite. Someone took over the child's body, hurting the child against his/her/their will, causing traumatic physical and/or psychic damage.

If Vanessa, an abuse survivor, plays out scenes where she is in control of what's happening, couldn't one argue that she is healing from the abuse, not replicating it? This offers a different perspective and alternative hypothesis, one that is often missing from psychological discourse. Letting one consider a healing versus harming hypothesis may feel like a bigger stretch when working with kink versus vanilla sex, but the challenge is worth the effort. It can take a lot of patience on a therapist's part to help a client, kink or vanilla, become curious about what their sexual preferences and activities mean to them. The NRST method has been instrumental in helping me navigate these issues.

We're All a Little Bit Kinky

The idea that people can master, rather than reenact, harmful experiences from the past through sex was a central belief of Robert Stoller (1979, 1985), a professor of psychiatry at UCLA medical school. Stoller was known for his theories concerning the development of gender identity and the dynamics of sexual excitement.

In the 1980s, people like Stoller and Ethel Spector Person were at the forefront of shifting perceptions of kink, away from the pathological to a more nuanced and accepting view. Prior to Stoller, therapists would analyze the childhoods of people who were gay or who had "perverted" sex to discover the childhood trauma that caused their sexual behavior in an attempt to change the perverted behavior, a reductionist approach at best.

Stoller studied sexual minority groups in San Francisco, people who were into bondage, urinating on their partners, and other atypical acts. He normalized and humanized their "perverse" behavior by putting it into the context of childhood wounds and the possibility of recovering from those wounds. What's called a "perversion" could serve a psychological function that's growth-enhancing.

One of Stoller's great insights is that we're all a little bit kinky, *if kink is defined not by the specific content of what we do sexually but what purpose it serves.* In *Observing the Erotic Imagination* (1985), he noted the following:

> I see the particular moment of erotic excitement as a tangled, compacted mass – a microdot – of scripts made up from impulses, desires, defenses, falsifications, truths avoided, and memories of past events, erotic and nonerotic, going back to infancy – a piece of theatre whose story seems genuine because of the truth of the body's sensations. Though the moment feels spontaneous, it is, rather, the result of years of working over the scripts in order to . . . ensure that they produce excitement, with its end product, gratification. I have pointed to . . . the importance of humiliation as a goad to creating the microdot and

as a hidden presence in the erotic moment. By *humiliation*, I mean the mechanism within the script that makes up the excitement, of revenge – humiliating another as payment for others having humiliated one.

(p. viii)

Stoller described sexual preferences, or "turn-ons," as attempts to cure the effects of traumas, frustrations, conflicts, and other painful conditions from childhood. I encourage all my clients to be curious about their sexual lives, whether they're into kink or not. What is the meaning or purpose of specific preferences? What is really being expressed? According to Stoller, all sexuality contains unconscious struggles with childhood dramas, therefore:

If my definitions confuse you because they imply that everyone is erotically aberrant and most people most of the time are at least a bit perverse, so be it.

(p. 9)

When Stoller said "most people most of the time are at least a bit perverse," what he meant was that our sexuality, however we practice it, is an attempt to resolve early childhood wounds. It's not about being a "little" bit kinky versus a "lot" kinky. It's not the difference between being gently tied down with scarves versus having hot wax poured on you. It's not about a continuum of sexual acts, from vanilla sex to BDSM. Rather, it's about the emotional and psychological meaning or purpose of *any* sexual act. Whether we have sex once a week in the missionary position or engage in extreme bondage, we're all dealing with attachment and trauma issues in the bedroom.

For Stoller, sexual excitement is as individual to a person as his/her/their fingerprints. A person's sexuality is a melodrama built on the tensions of risk, mystery, illusion, hostility, and revenge. During sex we become aroused when we can turn the traumas of early life into the triumph of sexual pleasure, offering the possibility for psychological growth. Since Stoller, stories of healing through BDSM experience continue to be poignantly described in contemporary psychotherapy work within the BDSM community (Moser & Kleinplatz, 2006; Ortmann & Sprott, 2013).

For sex therapist Jack Morin (1995), sexual excitement and the erotic experience are shaped by the push-pull of opposing forces. We are most intensely excited when we are a little off balance, uncertain, and poised on the perilous edge between ecstasy and disaster. The emotions we may think of as inhibiting arousal – shame, fear, guilt, anxiety, humiliation – may in certain people and contexts greatly enhance arousal.

As mentioned before, someone who is into polyamory might be judged by some therapists as being immature and commitment phobic. You could make the opposite argument that people who demand monogamy are overly jealous, too possessive, and more insecure than those who have a less rigid view of monogamy. Someone who can't manage monogamy might be insecure, but someone who demands monogamy may be equally insecure.

Sexuality is very complex and nuanced, and all sex is truly group sex because our histories are always operating in the bedroom. Therefore, we should all be curious about how our lifelong themes and narratives inform and create our sexual preferences, whether they be kink, vanilla, monogamous, or polyamorous. We should all want to engage with the past and uncover how it informs us as sexual beings now.

Discovering how one masters past wounds through one's sexuality involves identifying how one's sexual narratives inform sexual preferences and pleasures, and not judging them, but finding what works sexually as long as it's not coercive with anyone else.

Something as simple as missionary sex every Saturday night could contain psychological significance that's mostly unconscious. For example, maybe it feeds into a woman's need to be prioritized and desired by her husband in a way that her father was never able to provide. Her husband commits to her on schedule every week; he shows up and he gets hard and he has sex with her. This could involve mastery for the woman. It could help her heal from having a father who had no time for her on a Saturday or any other night of the week. Her derivative father, her husband, is making her feel important and desirable.

Why would this mastery be any different from a mastery achieved by her husband locking her in the basement dungeon and whipping her? Maybe her father hit her terribly when she was a kid. Now the man who's whipping her is someone she loves, someone she trusts. She has her safety word if she wants him to stop. Her body is into this. She likes it. She gets wet and aroused. She can choose the way her partner relates to her body. She has control. While it may feel similar to her childhood sensation of being hit, it contains a different psychological and relational context.

These examples demonstrate why it is so important for therapists to explore and engage the client's conscious and unconscious narratives. Most people don't realize what narratives are operating until we engage the NRST method to draw them out into the light.

What Defines Unhealthy Sexuality?

But can sexual acts also be harmful? Is there ever a time when I say to some-one, "I don't think you're gaining mastery"?

Absolutely, but my questioning is not based on the content of the act. It's based on the process of sex, how each member feels about themselves and the other before, during, and after sex. By this definition, once-a-week mission-ary sex can be unhealthy. For example, a husband has to have it that way and the wife just gives in. She's faking orgasms because she's afraid of hurting her husband's feelings. Her father abandoned her when she was five; she's afraid she's unlovable and that eventually her husband will abandon her as well. So she gives in to the husband. He always takes the lead and worries only about his pleasure, not hers; when he's done, he turns over and falls asleep. After-ward, she feels unloved, depressed, and drinks to the point of passing out.

When you start unpacking this sexual scene in an individual sexual his-tory session, the wife admits she's not even enjoying sex. She doesn't know who she is sexually. She's appeasing her husband in bed because she's afraid he'll leave her (like her father). It's important for me to question this kind of scene as a matter of course.

In my initial sessions with someone, I focus on the client's presenting problem and desire for change. If someone is practicing kink, I will explore it like any other sexual preference: "What was your first memory of sexual-ity? When did you become aware of your sexual preference? What do you do sexually? What works for you and your partner? What doesn't work?"

If a couple is having conventional "vanilla sex" once a week, they may not know that sex could be more pleasurable or intimate for them. They might resist opening up sexually because the way they have sex is more defensive than connected. It's not intimate or risk taking, in the sense that two peo-ple are revealing themselves to one another, are vulnerable, submit to one another, and explore new things. Sex just gets checked off the list.

That's why therapists shouldn't be fooled by mere sexual frequency. The *quality* of sex is more important. Frequency doesn't indicate or guarantee health or satisfaction. There could be significant psychological issues going on underneath the surface, known or unknown, that are not being addressed.

The Politics of Pathologizing S&M: What To Do About Power?

For a groundbreaking issue of *In the Family* magazine on "What Do Thera-pists Think About S&M," I was invited to be a discussant for an article on feminism, lesbians, and S&M. I was troubled by Carol Brockmon's article

(1998), "A Feminist View of Sadomasochism in the Nineties," that viewed all lesbian S&M behavior as problematic psychologically and politically, a view that echoed the troubled feminist Sex Wars in the 1980s, and one with which some therapists and clients still struggle.

One of Brockman's main criticisms is the unhealthy use of power roles in S&M relationships – one is the "top," one is the "bottom;" one is the Mistress, the other is the Slave; dangerous expressions of patriarchal domination and objectification. I am also concerned about the abuse of power in clients' relationships, but sometimes I wonder if we give "power" a bad name when it comes to the erotic, conflating erotic power with patriarchal abuses, when in truth power, per se, doesn't necessarily have to be toxic.

Because I am conscious of my own power in the therapeutic relationship, I realize that power is inherent in all relationships and can be used for good or bad. We have the power to make our partners feel deeply loved. We have the power to humiliate them, in or out of the bedroom. All relationships contain these possibilities because all relationships contain power inequalities – one person makes more money than the other; one is physically stronger than the other; one person may come from a more socially privileged group than the other.

Perhaps some therapists are uncomfortable with S&M because it concretizes the power inequalities of everyday life, the way that some people are uncomfortable with the way that drag queens parody feminine gender roles.

In whatever way S&M eroticizes power roles, what's important are the inner workings of the relationship: what kind of equality, respect, and consent are part of the erotic play? Attraction to people who are (or who are perceived to be) more or less powerful is a normal part of the human experience. After all, the first people we loved were our caregivers, who wielded enormous power over our bodies and our emotional wellbeing, and with whom we first experienced a variety of sensations and bodily pleasures. It is likely that all erotic exchanges include conscious and unconscious power dynamics, attractions and aversions, love and hostility. Our goal is to bring these dynamics to the fore and examine them, whatever our clients' sexual preferences might be.

Addressing Discrepant Kink Preferences

This issue comes to the forefront in couples when one partner was secretive about a kink preference throughout the relationship. It was never talked about. One partner indulged the preference and the other partner was in the dark about it. A crisis may ensue when the unsuspecting partner finds the "evidence," stockings behind the bed board, for example, and freaks out. For some people, discovering a partner's secret sexual indulgence is as much of a betrayal as an affair or discovering one's partner is gay when you thought they were heterosexual.

For some people, their kink preferences were even hidden from themselves. When that person comes out, a seemingly compatible vanilla sex couple now becomes a couple with discrepant sexual preferences. Secretive kink partners often need support to overcome their shame and internalized kinkphobia. Partners need help in working through negative narratives about kink and rebuilding trust in their erotic life.

The sex advice columnist and author Dan Savage has said that the best way to be a lover is through the three G's: striving to be good in bed, giving to the partner, and game for anything — within reason and mutually agreed upon.

Sometimes a non-kink partner is game to try their partner's favorite kink. The problem for some kink folks is that the real turn-on is when both people are equally excited by it. A partner may be willing and game, and get an A+ for generosity, but something is lacking for the kink partner. How do they address this discrepancy? If they wish to remain monogamous, I may explore with the kink partner whether masturbating or viewing kink porn may be fulfilling enough. The internet can be a resource for enjoying kink while remaining in a monogamous conventional sex relationship.

Or perhaps the couple can modify their monogamy agreement. Perhaps they can agree that the kink partner could visit a chat room or participate in online sex. Or once a month the partner can visit a kink club.

I worked with a gay couple, where one partner was into kink and the other partner was into anonymous sex. They had an agreement where, once a month, each was allowed to indulge his particular preference outside of the relationship. This was a totally open solution to their sexual differences.

Some people prefer kink sex but can also enjoy conventional sex. They can have an active sexual life with a primary partner, combined with some kink on the side with another partner in an open relationship arrangement. For some couples, that kind of arrangement when done with trust and transparency works well. It's built on the communication skills I've described earlier. However, if parameters for monogamy are narrow, discussion of managing sexual differences can take time.

My role as a therapist is to help people work out their differences without judgment. If shame isn't talked about and addressed, the kink person will keep preferences secret, sometimes creating distance in a relationship. That's worse for the couple than if they can bring the discrepancy out into the open and talk about it. During sexual history sessions, I conduct a deeper exploration with the kink partner about any issues of shame about their preference and how that affects sexuality with their partner.

Can the kink partner come out? Or will the kink preference be kept secret? Not all secrets are created equal. Not all secrets have a negative impact on a couple. For example, not everyone tells their partner what they fantasize about when they masturbate. These questions are important to explore during sexual history sessions.

If one partner can only function sexually with kink, and the other partner is only into conventional vanilla sex, that's a more challenging problem. Do they break up? Do they become a sexless relationship and outsource their sex? These are the kinds of challenges couples who have discrepant sexual preferences need to address.

Kink and the Coming-out Process

In our highly sexualized culture, after a book like *Fifty Shades of Grey* became a best-seller, you would think we've normalized most sexual practices, but that's not the case. Even today people who are into kink can still struggle with shame that they need to work through in order to come out and discuss it with a partner. If a non-kink partner is judgmental about kink, I take time either in couple sessions or in individual sexual history sessions to understand what negative narratives they are associating with kink. Sometimes, a partner's judgments involve aversions to the content of their partner's kink (i.e., feces, urine) that can be difficult to share for fear of hurting the partner's feelings. Quite often, someone with a kink interest partners with someone who doesn't share that interest. The kink partner either underestimates the importance of the kink in their life or tries to repress it. They often keep the kink preference compartmentalized or walled off from their partner until it finally gets revealed in some way. The kink person will often assume that hiding it will have little effect, but usually the desire either grows in power and/or eventually disrupts the relationship. A secret, separate sex life almost always affects the primary relationship.

The Case of Norman: If the Stocking Fits, Share It!

One client I worked with had a stocking fetish. Norman was married and had kids; his wife, Wendy, had no knowledge of his preference. He indulged his stocking fetish by masturbating with a pair of his wife's stockings. One day she discovered his stash of stockings and porn and freaked out, which brought them into therapy. His secret life felt like a complete betrayal to her. He didn't sleep with other women; it was all a fantasy life based on masturbating to porn, but for her it was just as bad as if he had had an affair. She wondered if her husband had an illness she just had to accept, like diabetes, or whether it was something deeper that she had to understand.

As I worked through Norman's sexual history, I found that his stocking fetish was linked to early memories of sitting by his mother's feet when she was eating. At age three or four, he would feel loved and loving by holding her legs, and even in adulthood he continued to associate stockings with those feeling of comfort and security. He adored his mother, but she didn't return the affection, so the only way he felt love and connection as a child was when she let him hold her legs.

Sharing about a fetish in a relationship can produce mixed results. It can increase intimacy but make sex challenging at first. Norman asked his wife to wear stockings early in their sexual life. She was fine with it until she heard his childhood associations to it. She felt she was his mother, not his wife, whenever they had sex, which inhibited her sexual enjoyment. She refused to wear stockings as a protest until she was sure it was she who he wanted, not his mother. This demonstrates how fraught and challenging the coming-out process can be.

However, over time as Norman's wife heard more about his emotional neglect as a child and witnessed his struggle to work through it, along with the shame he felt feeling unloved by his mother and keeping his fetish secret for so many years, she became more empathic about his attempt to master his childhood wound through his fetish.

"Why didn't you tell me about this when we first got together?" she implored. "You know I wouldn't have rejected you, not after all the loving support you gave me in the beginning."

This was true. Wendy was a survivor of date rape in college and had a very difficult time being touched in and out of bed. It took several years for Wendy to work through the effects of the assault.

"I was afraid you would reject me or lose your patience," she said. But Norman was gentle and kind to Wendy, telling her how moved he was that she shared her assault with him. She was always grateful for his generosity, and it eventually proved to be the safety she needed to open physically to another man.

"I could never do to you what my mother did to me," he said as he began to tear up. "I held you in my mind when you couldn't touch, and I was able to feel our love that way."

"Almost like the way you felt loved and loving as a child," I said. "Sounds like your fetish not only helped you heal, Norman, but it also enabled you to hold a space of healing for Wendy."

Both Wendy and Norman heard my reframe of the role his fetish played in their relationship, nodding and looking at each other. Words of gratitude followed. Norman looked a little sad. I asked why.

"I'm just sad that I didn't share my fetish with Wendy in the beginning. She's right. I spent a long time lonely, ashamed, and scared of being found out. She shared her pain with me. I should've shared mine with her," he said as he looked down. Wendy touched his hand.

If someone with a kink preference comes to me before being partnered, I often encourage them to connect with the kink community, even if only online. While I don't believe a kink person has to be partnered with another kink person, sharing the preference out in the open with other people reduces isolation and shame. Telling a potential partner during the dating phase makes a committed intimate relationship more possible. Without that openness and communication, remaining closeted with one's kink becomes a third in the relationship, limiting the intimacy and closeness that comes with being fully known.

My advice to therapists about working with kink varies, depending on how and when it emerges in therapy. If kink is revealed during the sexual history, the question I have to assess is whether it is secret or private. If the client isn't ashamed of it and can privately indulge it with masturbation or fantasy, it doesn't necessarily have to be disclosed or hurt the relationship. And, if the person is able to have a perfectly satisfying vanilla sex life with their partner, the kink can remain in the realm of private, just like any other masturbatory experience.

On the other hand, if kink is compulsively consuming the person's attention, if it's so shame-based that it affects sexual functioning with a partner, if they avoid partnered sex because masturbation is taking its place, or if they are seeking kink sex outside of a monogamous relationship, then my role is to determine the impact on the primary relationship. I work with the client to eventually bring the kink issue into the couple therapy. I may suggest some individual sessions to explore shame or conflict about the kink before integrating it into the couple therapy.

If kink is brought up spontaneously during couple therapy and/or the non-kink partner says it's a problem, then I address it as a difference in preferences and assess the level of distress in the couple. I will probe any conflicts or concerns about it and ask what each partner desires for their erotic life together.

Kink as Sexual Orientation

In her book *Sex With Shakespeare: Here's Much to Do With Pain, But More With Love*, author Jillian Keenan (2016) writes about how the Bard's plays helped her normalize and embrace her kink identity. Through an analysis of Shakespeare's works, Keenan demonstrates how he was "kink friendly." She does a very smart thing in this book, which is to hold off about her sexual history until later on, not wanting the reader to assume she was into kink because of some kind of abusive experience in her past.

When Keenan was ten years old, her mother punished her for an apparent transgression by striking her on the butt with a hairbrush.

> It felt like the most erotic part of my body was being violated against my will, in a way that was profoundly sexual to me – because that's exactly what was happening.
>
> (p. 231)

For the previous five years, Keenan had been "playing kinky games" of spanking sex-play with neighborhood kids. She already knew that her butt – "that big clitoris on the back of my pelvis" – had always been, by far, the most erotic part of her body.

Keenan's enraged mother spanked her frequently, which caused the young girl much confusion. Had her adult spanking fetish been caused by this early abuse?

> The closest reference points for my emerging sexual identity were things that had happened nonconsensually, and at my mother's hands.
>
> (p. 232)

Memories of being sexually titillated while spanked haunted Jillian for years, well into adulthood, with thoughts that her sexuality was "sick."

> What could have been – should have been – a source of pure pleasure had been poisoned. I felt, in the pit of stomach, that my fetish was *not*, as

conventional psychiatry would have me believe, the result of childhood trauma. But how could I deny that theory with such certainty when my own life seemed to confirm it?

(p. 234)

Over time, Keenan came to realize that it didn't really matter what caused her fetish.

It doesn't matter whether I was born with my sexuality intact, as I believe, or whether my fetish was imprinted early in my life by events I can or can't remember. What does matter is that sexuality – even non-normative sexuality – exists in children far earlier than most people want to admit. By the time I was three years old, I was a fetishist, and spanking, to me, was a sex act more penetrative than sex. From that point on, for me, nonconsensual spankings were unintentional sexual assaults.

(p. 238)

Keenan eventually achieved a powerful insight by age twenty-eight that freed her from haunted feelings that her childhood trauma caused her "sick" sexuality.

Trauma doesn't cause kink. But kink can cause trauma. In other words, if a child's innate sexuality is nonconsensually inflicted on her, trauma is a natural response.

(p. 242)

When her mother hit her, it felt at first like a sexual transgression. Keenan was also aware of being aroused, which was very confusing for her. This is similar to a sexual abuse or rape victim feeling physically stimulated during the violation. The victim will think: "What's wrong with me? Why would I have gotten hard or wet while I was being raped or molested?" A therapist's role is to help that person understand that such experiences do not mean that they wanted to be or enjoyed being violated.

While Keenan understands that being hit by her mother with a hairbrush is not the reason why she's into spanking today, you can make the argument, as Robert Stoller might, that spanking has helped her master her early abuse. Her kink existed before her mother began to spank her, but her kink was conflated and confused with that punishment. It wasn't until later in her life that she was able to separate the two and own her sexual preference separate from the abuse that happened to turn her on erotically.

A person with such an experience needs to work on her anger towards her mother and her conflicted feelings about her mother, as well as the confusion related to any sexual arousal while she was being abused. All of these feelings can influence someone's adult sexual life. But she is still going to like being spanked as she works through her childhood abuse.

Keenan's story is similar to Norman's. Touching his mother's stockings soothed him and provided a sense of nurturing and love. It was almost as if the stockings substituted for the parental love he never received. He wasn't abused but he was neglected, and the mastery of the loss was conflated with his eroticization of stockings. So you could say that parental or relational trauma was interwoven with the kink.

Did Norman have any other kind of stocking connections that weren't related to neglect? He did. As we further unpacked his story, I discovered that he was also attracted to his aunt's stockings, and she had been much kinder to him. His relationship with his mother was so complicated that we can't say for sure how or when his kink preference developed. How do we know how anyone's sexual preference comes to be? Stoller would say all sex is an attempt to repair trauma. He might say that Norman's stocking fetish originated in the trauma of having an unloving mother. So in this sense trauma helped create kink or became associated with it. While there might not be absolute causation, there could be association.

What's interesting about Keenan's story is that her mother's abuse felt like sexual abuse, and Keenan therefore associated her kink with trauma. Norman's stocking fetish was a secret, and it's often the secrecy of kink that can create trauma.

So we can say that kink creates trauma to the extent that society doesn't accept kink or the individual can't fully embrace that part of themself. Just as we have transphobia and homophobia, kinkphobia is also a reality.

As therapists, we have to leave open the question of how sexual preferences develop. Some recent research suggests that some kink can be considered a sexual orientation like gayness (Moser, 2016), when kink sexual attraction is strong and onset is reported in early childhood or adolescence. A relational sexual history should inquire about one's earliest memory of kink. If a client believes trauma created his/her/their kink, then I would follow that path and narrative. But ultimately that can be unpacked into a much broader set of conditions that go beyond trauma. The kink may have developed even in the absence of neglect or abuse. This is another example of how sexual narratives can be transformed.

Losing One's Kink

Some people who are into kink worry that if they examine the roots of their preference in therapy, they're going to "lose their kink" and diminish the excitement of the preference. In my experience as a sex therapist, I have never found that to happen.

If I explore, in a curious way, how a client's fascination with his mother's stockings led to his sexual preference, perhaps because he felt abandoned and unloved by his mother, the purpose is not to judge, pathologize, or fix such behavior but to understand it.

That therapy can't and shouldn't "cure" people of their preferences is illustrated by those clients who come to me with the desire to get rid of a kink preference. Perhaps they have a kink preference that is ruining their marriage. They're going to be kicked out of the house if they keep indulging it. But they can't stop doing it and ask me to cure them. I have to give them the bad news: that kind of preference is usually hard-wired early on. It's no more possible to change that preference than to change a homosexual person into a heterosexual person.

What I *can* do is help that person understand and reduce the shame about the kink. My approach is to work on healing early attachment wounds, not to get rid of the kink. He may then be able to relate to the kink differently. His arousal won't go away, but his kink might be less intrusive in his married sex life. Perhaps he no longer needs the kink every time he has sex with his wife. Perhaps he's a little less driven by, ashamed of, and obsessed with the kink. His wife might feel he's more present during sex. She may no longer feel he's more into the kink than he's into her. He's relating to her more as a whole person.

By exploring the underlying dynamics of kink, we don't do away with it. Rather, we explore possibilities for healing and growth, for better relations with partners and others. Kink, just like all sexuality in general, is an attempt to work through and master past traumas. If our sexuality didn't provide the outlet, we might never heal the wounds that shaped us.

The Importance of Kink Communities

When people who are into kink find like-minded communities, it can help them feel less isolated and ashamed. The importance of this cannot be understated, and the internet has been very helpful in creating kink communities. People in big cities can go to kink clubs, but for people in small or rural towns, the internet is what helps reduce their isolation.

For example, there is a website called Fetlife, where people with fetishes, BDSM, and other kink preferences can make contact with one another. It serves the same purpose that gay bars served in the 1950s and '60s.

One client, Harry, had a leather fetish. He became aroused by wearing leather chaps and vests and preferred to have sex dressed in leather. Harry, in his sixties when he entered therapy, was just beginning to make a narrative shift, viewing his kink as a preference instead of a perversion. He was still afraid to come out, convinced that his kink contributed to two past divorces. He was afraid that if he started dating again, women wouldn't accept his erotic "fixation" – his word.

I said to him, "Are you kidding me? There are a lot of women out there who would be into leather play." For now, I'm his kink-positive community since therapy is the only place he discusses his preference, but I'm hoping he will find a wider community where he can find other like-minded people and express his sexuality openly and without shame.

One thing that the kink community has to offer non-kink communities is their genuine respect for consent and clear guidelines. With their clear rules, kink clubs feel safer than bars. No drinking or drugs are allowed. "No" means "no." Kinksters, members of the community, use an acronym for consent: SSC, which means Safe, Sane, and Consensual.

Some clients aren't ready to go to a kink club. One man I worked with couldn't bring himself to visit the Fetlife website. But the fact that such websites exist can be very reassuring and empowering for people; the resource is there when they're ready to use it. These resources can help clients with self-acceptance, coming out, and dealing with feelings of shame or rejection. They can communicate with like-minded people and eventually find friends and partners. And therapists should regard kink internet resources as part of their own sex education. If you're working with a kink client, I recommend you go online and become familiar with Fetlife and other similar websites to identify what arouses you and what repels you so you can manage your countertransference to kink. You owe it to your clients.

CHAPTER 9

☀

GEORGE AND MARTHA TRY TO HAVE SEX
Listening to Emotional Sadism

One day a couple came into therapy, and I asked them my standard opening question: "What brings you here?"

Ed pointed to his wife Sally and said, "Well, look at her." I glanced at Sally, looked back at him, and asked: "What do you mean?"

In a curt tone he repeated, "Well, look at her," as if his meaning was obvious.

"Well, when I look at her," I replied, "what am I supposed to see?" She was a very attractive woman and, as I would soon learn, a successful artist. But from the get-go, Ed had complete contempt for her. He relentlessly disparaged everything about Sally – from the way she dressed, to the way she did her hair, to the way she talked. Her every aspect elicited his disgust. She was the reason, he claimed, he had no sexual desire and couldn't get aroused.

It was painful to hear Ed disparage her. But as much as I was thinking, "Oh my God, this poor woman," another part of me was saying, "But this woman stayed married to him for ten years. What's her story? Why does she tolerate his emotional abuse? What is she trying to work out by being with a man who treats her like that?"

In other words, there was a balancing narrative to Sally's role as a "victim." Whenever I encounter a couple where one partner plays the tormenting sadist and the other the suffering masochist, there is always more beneath the surface than what first seems obvious. In a sense, I don't believe in merely masochism as an explanation in situations like this. Rather, the "masochistic" partner, by staying and playing her role with the "sadist," allowing him to talk to her in that way and not fighting back, is (as we've seen in earlier case examples) trying to work out something from childhood. My job as therapist is to follow the relational trail of breadcrumbs through the historical forest to get to the emotional truth of the situation, for both partners.

The first part of following the trail is to conduct the relational sexual histories. What happened in Ed's past to make him so full of rage? What kind of neglect or abuse did he suffer? In Ed's case, he had a mother who had no interest in being a mother. People who do not have a satisfying bond with their caregivers in infancy and childhood inevitably develop all sorts of contorted ways of experiencing attachment in their adult lives. One manifestation of that contortion can be emotional sadism in partnered relationships, the focus of this chapter.

Defining Emotional Sadism

What is emotional sadism and why devote an entire chapter to it in this book?

Even the best marriages or relationships have conflict, because conflict is inevitable between human beings. Emotional sadism, however, is several steps beyond the normal conflict and aggression that most people experience.

Psychologist David Schnarch (1991), in his book *Constructing the Sexual Crucible*, talks about "normal marital sadism." It's normal for a wife to say about her husband, "I hate my husband. I hate him because he reminds me of the worst parts of my father." This is important, because some couples can't imagine that hatred is a normal thing to feel. When I tell them that it is, their reaction is usually, "Oh, really?" But if someone doesn't allow for feelings of dislike or hatred for a partner, those feelings go underground and come out in other, more harmful ways. There's nothing wrong with having those feelings at certain points with a partner.

At the same time, I want to differentiate here between Schnarch's "normal marital sadism" and malevolent emotional sadism, which is not a state couples go in or out of, but rather a way of being. Emotional sadism is an entrenched, co-created dynamic of sadism/masochism that becomes the only way a couple relates and feels connected.

In a non-emotional sadism couple, one partner might give the other partner the silent treatment after a perceived hurt, but the next night they're making love again. In other words, *they can recover after a rupture*. In contrast, emotional sadism involves getting pleasure from emotionally harming someone, far different from the usual hurts we cause one another in most relationships. There is no recovery process. The couple lives in a state of rupture they carefully choreograph. The emotionally sadistic pattern feels familiar to clients because they are playing out what parents did to each other or what one of their parents did to them. Whatever the early pattern was, it's being reenacted in the present romantic relationship.

While intense emotions come to the surface in any relationship, they tend to be of a different order of difficulty in an emotionally sadistic relationship. Included is an intention to harm the other and derive pleasure from inflicting that harm. With true emotional sadism, the dynamic between the two partners is exquisitely interwoven, with one partner playing the sadist and the other playing the masochist at any given time, often as a defense against marital intimacy and sexuality. It's a very difficult kind of couple dynamic with which to work.

At the same time, it's important not to pathologize emotional sadism, as homosexuality, kink, and other sexual behaviors have been pathologized in the past. While emotional sadism is not pretty to witness in action, it's not a behavior that should be vilified. As always, my goal as a therapist is to illuminate and understand the behavior.

Emotional Sadism and Early Childhood Nurturing

What most emotionally sadistic people didn't receive in childhood was the "gleam in the mother's eye," a term coined by psychoanalyst Heinz Kohut. It's worth repeating what Kohut had to say about this concept in *The Restoration of the Self* (1977):

> The child that is to survive psychologically is born into an empathic-responsive human milieu (of self-objects) just as he is born into an atmosphere that contains an optimal amount of oxygen if he is to survive physically. And his nascent self "expects" . . . an empathic environment to be in tune with his psychological need-wishes with the same unquestioning certitude as the respiratory apparatus of the newborn infant may be said to "expect" oxygen to be contained in the surrounding atmosphere.
>
> (p. 85)

In such an environment, the child gets to participate in the "glow of pride and joy that emanates from the parental self-objects." Nurturing caregivers, Kohut notes, are open to that "empathic merger with their children that would allow them to delight in their children's growth and assertiveness . . . to be able to experience the growth of the next generation with unforced non-defensive joy" (p. 237).

When someone doesn't receive "the gleam in the mother's eye," they develop a complicated relationship to desire. They can't move into willingness easily, either as the subject or object of it, because not experiencing desire in either form is too painful a reminder of the love and attention they didn't receive in childhood.

A caregiver's warmth and attention is the first primary connection that helps us feel desired and desirable. That connection is the first time a child is seen and loved for who they really are. If they experience their caregiver's attunement, they feel valued and learn how to regulate their feelings. This kind of mirroring forms a child's emotional foundation; without that foundation, one develops contorted ways of seeing and experiencing attachment. In Ed's case, his mother rejected him. She wasn't a happy mother and paid him and his siblings very little attention. In his adult life he chose to reject the woman in his life rather than become the rejected child all over again.

Emotional sadism can manifest itself in all kinds of relationships. It can happen in same-sex relationships as well as heterosexual ones. Men can do it to women and women can do it to men. One stereotype is that the man is always the sadistic aggressor and the woman is invariably the suffering masochist, but that isn't always the case. There is also a stereotype that gays and lesbians, having felt the sting of societal rejection and injustice, would stick together in comfort and solidarity, leaving no room for displays of emotional sadism with one another. However, one only needs to look to artistic works like the films *Boys in the Band* or *The Children's Hour* to be disabused of that belief. In fact, those films poignantly provide examples of emotional sadism that result from internalized homophobia and self-hatred. Even if LGBTQ people are lucky enough to experience caregivers with a degree of "gleams in the eye" in general, many still experience familial and/or societal absence of mirroring non-normative sexual and gender experience.

Psychoanalyst Peter Fonagy, in his 2008 article "A Genuinely Developmental Theory of Sexual Enjoyment and Its Implications for Psychoanalytic Technique," locates the source of adult sexual dysregulation in the absence of the early childhood "mirroring":

> Because emotional regulation arises out of the mirroring of affect by a primary caregiver and sexual feelings are unique in that they are systematically ignored and left unmirrored by caregivers, sexual feelings remain fundamentally dysregulated in all of us.

(p. 11)

Fonagy makes the point that all childhood sexuality is unmirrored by caregivers since there exists so little guidance about how to properly mirror childhood sexuality. When one adds the degree of homophobia and transphobia in families and society, one can appreciate the additional amount of sexual/gender misattunement some LGBTQ clients endured in childhood that in certain cases can contribute to emotional sadism in adult relationships.

The Case of Michael and Lance: Internalized Homophobia Played Out Through Emotional Sadism

A highly accomplished gay couple, Michael and Lance, entered couple sex therapy to improve communication, reduce constant bickering, and improve their sex life. Their relational sexual histories revealed that many of their issues stemmed from painful gay-boy childhoods. Neither experienced parental abuse, but they experienced continual bullying and ridicule from other boys about their "sissy-boy" ways and lack of athletic prowess. They suffered in silence, never telling their parents, none of whom would have offered solace or support. They kept their developing gay identities secret from their parents, siblings, and friends. Both of them emerged from childhood feeling ashamed and defective, unmirrored in their true selves. Both engaged in heterosexual dating in college as attempts to deal with their insecurities about masculinity, while hooking up with men on the side, creating a split-off, shameful, separate gay sexual life.

They were both quite brilliant in their chosen professions and were immediately attracted to each other intellectually when they met in their thirties. One was an accomplished architect, the other a famous interior designer. It was a perfect marriage, career-wise. Even though they didn't work together on projects, their worlds overlapped, and they created what some gay men call a "fabulous lifestyle."

In his book *The Velvet Rage: Overcoming the Pain of Growing Up Gay in a Straight Man's World*, Alan Downs (2012) writes about "the fabulous gay man." Attractive, usually well-off, owning a beautiful apartment, collecting great art work, wearing beautiful clothing, and always flying first class. Everything has to be perfect, and the fabulous gay man often has contempt for others who don't match up to his level of perfection. But, Downs wonders, isn't this a very tightly woven package designed to defend against underlying shame, harm, and wounding about homosexuality?

Michael and Lance had this kind of defensiveness woven into their "fabulousness." They didn't know how to create intimacy based on authenticity and vulnerability. They would take turns performing the perfect emotional S&M ballet. If one of them began to talk about something vulnerable (read: imperfect), the other would use it against him like a weapon, which would make the first partner close off and find something with which to wound the other one. They rarely agreed on anything, engaging in huge arguments about where to hang a painting or where to go on vacation. I considered assigning *The Velvet Rage* as part of therapy with them, but given their use of intellectualization as a defense, therapy had to bypass the intellectual to get to a more vulnerable affective level.

Their shared defense against vulnerability played out in their sex life, as well. They never communicated their sexual preferences to each other despite being together for fifteen years; it felt too risky to even ask. The chance of reliving bully-boy ridicule or rejection was too high. They began to live unspoken parallel non-monogamous lives. They didn't have a contract; if one of them was on a business trip or out of town, they did what they felt like doing. Eventually they weren't having any sex in the relationship, and that's when they came in to see me.

Both felt rejected that the other never initiated sex anymore, but neither of them could express it openly and directly. They felt ashamed because their fabulous male friends were having sex and they weren't. They didn't like sitting at a dinner table with an open secret between them that made them feel more like brothers than lovers.

Identifying and discussing their vulnerabilities in individual sexual history sessions set the stage to begin working with each of them to transform their sadistic and contemptuous feelings into expressions of deeper vulnerability and desire. They needed the safety and empathic container of the individual sessions to identify and articulate the wounds from the past. I normalized the challenges and defenses of gay boys left to their own devices to survive anti-gay, hyper-masculinized environments. Having identified and externalized these problems, they were ready to begin articulating the needs under their defenses in couple sessions. I helped the process with interventions that reduced shame about their defenses and encouraged deeper communication.

For example, I would say after one of them delivered a particularly cruel comment:

"Sounds like right now you're experiencing your partner as one of those bully-boys from school so you're going on the offensive."

Eventually followed by:

"What need is underneath that comment?"

As you might imagine, the process took a very long time, explaining and normalizing the development of their defenses, how they protected them as tortured sissy-boys, but now barricaded them from the love and intimacy they crave with each other. Part of our process was to use the sexual history stories and narratives to identify the abuse they experienced at the hands of the other boy that was now projected onto the other. We spent a lot of time working through their childhood wounds together. As they gradually developed empathy, they began to be better peers to each other than their school peers had been to them. As their defensiveness diminished, they were able to express their needs for acceptance, love, and closeness.

The Emotional Sadism of George and Martha in
Who's Afraid of Virginia Woolf?

When I give workshop presentations to therapists, and mention that I've worked with a real "George and Martha couple," heads nod and people smile nervously. Everyone understands what I mean. George and Martha are the exquisitely malevolent couple in the great film adaptation of Edward Albee's play *Who's Afraid of Virginia Woolf?* Anyone who has seen the electrifying performances by Richard Burton and Elizabeth Taylor has witnessed an unforgettable display of raw and unfettered emotional sadism.

It may seem like Martha is the wretch, the bitch, the difficult one, but they are true equals in their ability to dish it out and take it. Taylor and Burton capture the entrenched dynamic that makes these couples so difficult to work with, even if alcoholism weren't a factor. They present a different dynamic from the typical non-emotionally sadistic couple who get bored, irritated, or angry with one another. In "George and Martha couples," emotional sadism becomes a relational third, a living part of the relationship. Such a couple will fight to the death to keep the dynamic going. They often don't have the inner emotional resources to disrupt it.

I was working with a couple who was caught in this dynamic, who hadn't had sex in years. At one point I gave them a homework assignment to watch the film *Who's Afraid of Virginia Woolf?* The wife's face lit up. "Oh, that's my favorite movie!"

I almost fell out of my chair, but she wasn't kidding. They went home to watch the film and compare themselves to George and Martha. In the next session they told me, in a very sober way, "Oh my God, that couple *really* has problems. We're not *that* bad." In a way, watching the film helped them begin to appreciate good parts of their relationship.

At one point after the wife listed all of her husband's failures, I said to her, "If you don't mind me asking, if there are so many things you don't like about him, so much neglect that takes place every day, why do you stay with him?"

"Oh, because he's a good man," she replied. And she meant it. One minute she would tear him down as passive and weak, or because he didn't help enough around the house, or because he never told her she was beautiful. But she would never leave him.

This couple had perfected their emotional sadism, she as the sadist and he as the masochist. But, like George and Martha, they could easily switch roles at the drop of a hat. At one point, Martha says, "George who is good to me, and whom I revile, who keeps learning the games we play as quickly as I can change the rules" (Albee, 2005, pp. 201–202). Martha might look like she has the upper hand because she's the louder one, belittling George in front of the guests, but George, although quieter, gets right back at her, killing their imaginary child at the film's end. She breaks down, and you can tell he enjoys it. Then he's patting her and comforting her, saying that it will be okay, but he knows it's checkmate and he's got her in a corner. He dropped the final straw that broke her back and got pleasure from doing so.

Martha also reveals a deeper source of emotional sadism, that of self-loathing. She continues:

> George . . . whom I will not forgive for having come to rest; for having seen me and having said: yes, this will do; who has made the hideous, the hurting and the insulting mistake of loving me and must be punished for it.

> (p. 202)

Emotional sadism often has at its core self-loathing and self-hatred. Ed, whose mother wished he was never born, felt on some level that he was unwanted, the untouchable physically and emotionally. In this toxic relational soil, his child mind sprouted a secret narrative to make sense of it all – that he was too hateful to be loved, too disgusting to be touched. And whomever dared to love him, Sally in this case, had to be punished.

Sexual Dynamics in an Emotionally Sadistic Couple

I view couples as systems that create particular dynamics that sustain it. A sadist can't exist without a masochist, and vice versa. The sadist and the masochist can change roles back and forth, sometimes within a split second. They change roles fluidly; no one partner is the "victim." *The co-created dynamic victimizes the couple.*

This sadism, of course, infects the couple's sexual dynamic. If the woman is "the witch" constantly attacking her husband, he can make her feel totally undesirable in the bedroom. Even if he has sex with her, he can do it in a disconnected way that has nothing to do with really seeing her, relating to her only to get what he wants. Sadism can be subtly expressed in a passive-aggressive way, where one partner refuses to initiate sex or doesn't respond to the partner's expressions of sexual desire.

In one scene in *Who's Afraid of Virginia Woolf?*, George and Martha are on the bed laughing with each other in a way that seems to create a shared intimacy for a split second. Martha then lies on top of George and says, "Come on, kiss me." The mood shifts as he contemptuously pushes her away, refusing the invitation, a rare intimate moment ruptured, returning the couple dynamic to its antagonizing homeostasis.

With emotional sadism, couples are creating a kind of ruthless power differential that in more functional couples could contribute to a good sex life. In non-emotionally sadistic couples, playing with power is ultimately for the sake of sexual pleasure. It occurs within a context of intimacy and safety. In contrast, the emotional sadism of George and Martha is not for the purpose of pleasure or sexual connection. Emotional sadism rarely contributes to a satisfying sex life. The partners are too undifferentiated to manage it. There are no scenes in the film of pleasurable sexual interaction between Martha and George. Instead, Martha goes off and has sex with their guest, Nick, as a way of mocking and punishing George.

Part of what makes sexuality fulfilling is being able to surrender and be vulnerable. Good sex comes from feeling one's need for the other and admitting even to oneself that one is dependent on the partner to complete one's pleasure. These emotional skills are too vulnerable for people who are ensnared in emotional sadism, who don't experience enough emotional safety interpersonally or intrapsychically to take erotic risks.

Listening to Emotional Sadism With NRST: Making the Transformation to an Erotic Connection

Emotional sadism is about unfinished business from the past. The hardest cases are where couples are attempting to work out issues from before the couple even met. This was the case with Ed, whose mother hardly recognized his presence when he walked into a room. There was no gleam in his mother's eye. In fact, I asked him directly: "If your mother's eyes had spoken, what would they have said to you?"

His reply: "I'm so sorry you were born."

I helped him understand the emotional cost to him of that childhood. At one point I said to him, "It sounds like you wish your *wife* was never born. You're making Sally feel the same way that your mother made you feel."

I went further and told him that there was a defensive aspect to his behavior. Ed would rather attack his wife than run the risk that she didn't have affection for him. It was his way of defending against being ignored, as his mother once did to him. His sadism protected him from feeling that enormous childhood loss.

When I said that to Ed, he cried.

This is the family of origin work at the core of NRST. I'm searching for those deep relational roots that contribute to the presenting sexual problem. A client may replicate what they experienced in childhood, or they may defend against it, as it was in Ed's case. What was poignant for me was that Sally had a great deal of affection for Ed despite all of the abuse.

"What a shame," I said to him. "You married a woman who has the affection for you that your mother never had, and yet you can't feel it and you do everything you can to push her away." This was very painful for Ed to take in, but eventually he did.

I also explored Sally's role in the relationship. Why did she allow herself to be subject to Ed's sadism? Through the relational sexual history, I learned that she had a malevolent mother who had once said to her "I wish you were not my daughter" and who refused to attend important milestones in Sally's life, her college graduation and her wedding. After all that, Sally would still call her mother regularly to check in with how she was doing. Sally developed a high tolerance for criticism. She equated attachment with emotional rejection.

How did her past factor into their sadistic-masochistic dynamic? She could have told her mother to go to hell. Or she could have said, "I'm never coming to your funeral." But she didn't. She remained faithful to her mother despite the rejection, and she repeated this pattern in her marriage to Ed. Her mother was sadistic, and she replicated it with a partner who was the same way.

Ed and Sally were able to work through a lot of their issues in therapy. Ed's parents were dead, but Sally was able to eventually confront her mother about the past and construct a different way of relating to her going forward.

Emotionally Sadistic Transference

All sex therapy is also couple therapy. It's impossible to separate sex from couple dynamics, so for me there's no separation between sex therapy and "regular" couple therapy. I integrate psychodynamic and couple systems work into NRST, along with cognitive behavioral sex therapy approaches.

A behavioral sex therapist who never had any psychoanalytic or couple systems training would probably refer an emotionally sadistic couple like Ed and Sally to a couple therapist. Since a large amount of the treatment involves working with unconscious childhood material, cognitive behavioral work is not enough, or may not even be possible, at least in the initial stage of therapy.

When I give homework assignments to more seriously distressed emotionally sadistic couples, they usually reject them. They often express contempt for the idea of "homework" (and for me for suggesting it), and can become emotionally sadistic toward me, making comments like, "You haven't helped us at all," or more pointedly, "We thought you knew how to help couples with their sex life."

It takes a certain amount of secure attachment and safety for a couple to engage in a homework assignment together. Some couples can't tolerate the degree of trust and connection required. They instead have to work on their individual issues before they can engage in behavioral homework assignments or creating sexual menus. With these kinds of couples, my work becomes more couple therapy than sex therapy at first in order to create a strong enough foundation of safety, trust, and communication before they can work toward a more fulfilling sexual connection.

If one or both partners haven't had individual therapy, I might suggest that they do so while we work in couple sex therapy. It can be very helpful to have a therapeutic "team approach" to achieve the emotional and sexual goals. More often, both partners have already been in individual psychotherapy or psychoanalysis because their emotionally sadistic patterns have wreaked havoc in other areas of their lives, such as trouble in the workplace or in their families.

By working with each partner's sexual histories, I help identify the narratives connected to their families of origin and how their patterns of emotional sadism developed in response to those childhood experiences. Sometimes they're reenacting what their parents did to them. Other times the sadism is a way of managing something from the past that wasn't so overtly sadistic, but had more to do with rage about neglect or lack of attunement. Either way, by listening carefully to emotional sadism and not being repelled by it, I'm able to help couples establish more healthy ways of relating to one another.

Maintaining Therapeutic Boundaries With a Sadistic Couple

With every couple a therapist has to maintain boundaries, but an emotionally sadistic couple poses particular challenges. One huge challenge is to guard against the contagiousness of sadism. It's tempting for the therapist to want to be sadistic toward one or both partners because they can be so frustrating. Therapists can lose their calmness and become emotionally dysregulated. You can fail to be as empathic or as patient as you need to be. You can get into what I call "an enactment" with a couple, where the therapist becomes the sadist or the couple joins together to attack the therapist. You may unconsciously play victim (masochist) by apologizing for failing them. The couple can then derive sadistic pleasure from having colluded to engage and ensnare you into their enmeshed dynamic (Willi, 1977). It can feel like a complicated undertow that's fraught with danger if one doesn't know how to resist their draw.

Painful sessions are often when both partners join forces to attack the therapist. Luckily, those times are rare. When it does happen, it sometimes makes the couple closer than they've been in a long time because at least they've joined against someone else instead of tormenting each other. But it's not pleasant for the therapist.

The therapist carries his/her/their own emotional/sexual narratives and history, and being aware of those narratives is crucial in maintaining proper therapeutic boundaries. This is true in working with all couples, but especially true with emotional sadism, which has greater potential for disrupting the therapeutic process.

It's understandable for a therapist to get triggered more by the sadist than by the masochist. You can become uncomfortable, even guilty, watching one person debase or show contempt for the other. It's often difficult to sit by and watch what looks like emotional abuse. As a therapist, it's important to tell yourself, "There are no victims or villains here, even though it really looks like one person is victimizing the other. Let me let some time elapse so I can more clearly see the dynamic they are co-creating before disrupting it."

What is the therapist's ethical responsibility here? When do you step in and say, "Hey, wait a minute, you really shouldn't be talking to her/him/them that way"?

That direct a statement is not my style (though I may be feeling it inside); instead I would ask a question like I did with Michael and Lance:

"What request do you have for your partner under that comment?"

Armed with knowledge of the client's childhood wounds and narratives, I could add an empathic statement to my question that speaks to the hurt child part underneath the contemptuous adult part.

The Importance of Sexual Self-Awareness for Therapists

When I talk about sexual self-awareness, that applies to therapists as well as clients. Having a healthy sense of sexual self-awareness enables therapists to keep their boundaries, to avoid judging their clients, and to work effectively with people who might be treating each other in ways that seem repellent or repugnant. A therapist can't be successful in their work if they aren't aware of their own sexual and emotional turn-offs and triggers.

It's very important that we normalize countertransference, because it happens all the time in therapeutic work. A therapist must be aware of weak points, our Achilles' heel(s). To do so, we need to engage in sexual self-awareness, to identify and own our sexual history and narratives. Failing to do so can lead to problematic dynamics in therapy, where your history and your client's histories conflict or intertwine in unconscious and destructive ways.

In working with emotionally sadistic couples, the therapist has to be very careful not to become the villain (or the victim) or take on the sadist, because that will simply result in the sadist or masochist turning on you with hatred and contempt. It can feel like an emotional three-card monte. It's intense work; how do you stay regulated and not split your feelings about the partners into "good" or "bad"? How do you play neither the sadistic nor masochistic role? How do you manage when the couple teams up against you? This requires being aware of your own relational history of feeling excluded, criticized, or ridiculed. The more dysregulated we become with clients, the more it's possible their dynamics are hitting a personal emotional nerve.

And, more generally, how do we handle the sexual turn-ons, attractions, and aversions of our clients? When I sit with clients who share information about their sexual lives with me, I observe and contain my own value judgments long enough to inquire about what their sexual experiences mean to them and to their relationships. The criteria I use to assess problematic sexual behavior are based on the *quality* of the sexual relationship and the distress that clients experience. This is my own value system in therapy: healthy sexuality is determined by the connection it engenders between partners. These criteria help me resist being distracted by the method of sexual pleasuring. I am alert for signs that a sexual act is more important than the partner, or that there is a fixed, compulsive quality to the sexual act. If a ritualized sexual act is the only way a client can achieve pleasure, then I explore the possible problematics of that rigidity for the client and/or the partner.

Every therapist has a bottom line, and there are clients we can't work with. If we can't hold a space non-judgmentally and become overwhelmed by the content, we aren't the right therapist for those clients. We need to know our limits, values, and beliefs. To me, this is the most important thing we can do when we are working across differences. We should remember what Fonagy said on this subject (emphasis mine):

> Because emotional regulation arises out of the mirroring of affect by a primary caregiver and sexual feelings are unique in that they are systematically ignored and left unmirrored by caregivers, *sexual feelings remain fundamentally dysregulated in all of us.*
>
> (p. 11)

In addition to your classroom training and case supervision, there is also a Sexual Attitude Reassessment (SAR) experience, which is standard training to become a certified sex therapist. Therapists in training spend an entire weekend flooded by diverse kinds of sexual material, which they then process in group sessions. You are able to determine your weak points by identifying what material triggers and dysregulates you.

You can also use this book to examine your sexual history and narratives. You can conduct your own sexual history. Ask yourself: what's your earliest memory of sexuality and of gender development? What kinds of talks did your parents have with you about sex? How did you learn about sex? What was your masturbation history? Your relationship history?

If you have a partner, you can construct a sexual menu together. You can explore sensate focus and mindfulness during sex. If you're single, you can explore your sexuality, too. I will discuss this further in the next chapter.

Make a list of topics a client might bring into session that would have the greatest chance of dysregulating you. Is your discomfort about gay issues? Trans issues? About certain sexual practices? Anal sex? Pain? What sexual roles or attitudes trigger discomfort? Humiliation? Domination? What particular questions from a client would be hard for you to answer? Where do you find yourself becoming judgmental about certain sexual or relationship choices?

By asking and answering these questions, you'll be better able to address whatever issues arise with clients without losing your grounding. Use this book not only as a guide to working with clients, but as a guide to exploring and understanding your own sexual self.

CHAPTER 10

✺

SEXUAL RESILIENCE

Maintaining an Erotic Connection to Self and Other(s)

Everyone is an erotic being, and that includes people who don't have a partner. A lot of people feel they aren't erotic beings until they're with someone sexually, but that's a very limiting view of eroticism. Black lesbian feminist poet Audre Lorde (1984), in her essay *Uses of the Erotic: The Erotic as Power*, expands our understanding of the erotic by describing it as a creative life-force empowering us to be more intentionally alive and joyful in the world. She writes:

> The erotic is a measure between the beginnings of our sense of self and the chaos of our strongest feelings. It is an internal sense of satisfaction to which, once we have experienced it, we know we can aspire. For having experienced the fullness of this depth of feeling and recognizing its power, in honor and self-respect we can require no less of ourselves.
>
> (p. 54)

I often introduce to clients the concept of intentional pleasure, broadly defined, as embracing a spirit of willingness into a person's solo erotic and relational life. As with couples, it displaces sexual desire, as the essential motivation for erotic exploration. Sexual desire is so mysterious; it can wax and wane, and when it wanes in couples, the relationship begins to buckle under the weight of a plethora of negative narratives. When it wanes in a single person, they might feel they've entirely lost their sexuality, and thus retire from the world of the erotic in general. With singles as well as couples, willingness enables someone to have a robust and continuous erotic life whether or not they are single or in a sexless relationship.

While this chapter is primarily for singles, it's important to remember that couples consist of two single people and sometimes become too merged. Their lives depend so much on the relationship, they can give their partner too much responsibility for their sexual self-esteem and erotic pleasure. They often lose sight of their sexual agency.

"Intentional" is a concept I borrow from Buddhism, in the sense that we possess the potential for awareness and responsibility for ourselves. We're not putting the responsibility for enjoyment or pleasure on the other. We create and can re-create our individual reality, which informs the basis of a narrative approach to sexuality. It's crucial that we become aware of what narratives we're telling ourselves and living with, consciously or unconsciously, whether or not we're in a partnered relationship.

Becoming intentional about one's erotic life is no different or less important than becoming intentional about what one eats, how much one exercises, or how one takes care of emotional or spiritual well-being. You're facing and taking responsibility for the narratives you've internalized or constructed, the influences of your family and society, and for creating new and better narratives going forward.

Sexual agency and intentional pleasure can help overcome conditioning we've received – about being single, having been indoctrinated by religion, having been traumatized in some way, or experiencing conflicted feelings about sexuality due to a wide range of personal, relational, and social factors. The idea that someone doesn't deserve (sexual) pleasure may not be a conscious thought, but could be an underlying unconscious narrative that a client has been carrying around for a long time. Our goal as therapists is to help identify and transform our clients' anti-pleasure narratives.

Sexuality Is Literally Our Birthright

We have a sexual birthright just by being born. Little babies are sensual beings, if you define part of sexuality as sensation in the body. The minute a child is born, it begins its neurological, psychological, emotional, and physical experiences. Our bodies get stimulated, and we both give and receive pleasure, starting in infancy.

If a caregiver is providing the appropriate attunement and nurturing, the baby feels satiated. When the baby cries and is attended to and fed, the baby's sensory system is alive with pleasure. And the baby's whole emotional/sensory system is alive the minute it begins to interact with caregivers. Is the baby fulfilled and satiated in the right ways, at the right times, and with the right feelings by the caregiver? What is the quality of the emotional connection? That template is established at a very young age and forms the foundation for our sexuality, our ability to give and receive pleasure later on.

Research has found that babies masturbate very early on, finding pleasure in their genitals (Schiedel, 2018). As adults we have to remind ourselves of this sexual birthright, that we are sexual beings and can take responsibility for our pleasure, and this includes everyone, also people with disabilities (PWD). If you have a body, you can experience sensual/emotional pleasure, no matter how well one's parts function. It is important for therapists to be culturally competent when working with PWD, assessing sexual functioning and conducting sexual histories to identify misconceptions and negative narratives about disability and sexual health (Mona, Cameron, & Cordes, 2017).

Hedonism Anyone?

One characteristic I explore with clients is how pleasure-seeking, or hedonistic, they are, assessing their ability to experience and enjoy pleasure. How much pleasure do they have in life in general, not just sexually? Listening for how clients describe pleasure-seeking is diagnostic. Here are some words clients have used in sessions:

- Guilty pleasures
- Selfish indulgences
- Undisciplined
- Wasting time
- Not accomplishing anything
- Feeling lazy
- Excessive
- Extravagant

These anti-pleasure values and their underlying narratives, "If I experience pleasure, I will become insatiable," for example, often contribute to clients' struggles with experiencing partnered pleasures. Few clients make the connection that one of the reasons they might not be enjoying sex is that they don't know how or don't feel comfortable with enjoying anything in life. It may sound obvious, but some clients need help in seeing the connection between the two.

In this case, I often start a menu or mindfulness assignment focusing on non-sexual or even non-physical items to expand a person's capacity to experience pleasure in general. I explore with the client(s) what to call the menu: Fun Menu, Pleasure Menu, Enjoyment Menu, as possibilities. As with narrative mindful touch, I might ask them to write about their thoughts, feelings, or bodily sensations while experiencing a pleasure menu item, often providing a path to identifying deeper narratives.

I also make the connection between non-sexual pleasures and sex. If someone enjoys exercise, they get on their bicycle every morning. That person experiences bodily pleasure and emotional satisfaction. They bring a thoughtfulness and intentionality to their daily exercise routine. They get on the bike even if they are tired because they know that they're going to feel better afterward. They are intentional about seeking and experiencing pleasure through exercise.

The same attitude can apply to sexual pleasure. Some people bring more intentionality to seeking and experiencing sexual pleasure than others. This underscores the issue of willingness versus desire. Just as someone gets on their bicycle when they don't feel like it, someone who is intentional about exploring sexual pleasure could be willing to have sex even if they're tired or not experiencing desire. They bring intentionality to seeking sexual pleasure, and afterward are often glad they did.

Reframing the Past and Developing Sexual Agency

As is made clear throughout this book, NRST is based on helping clients reframe their experiences. Reframing offers a different, positive way of seeing something. It raises a client's curiosity about the frames or assumed narratives they've constructed about themselves. Once a client can expand their view of self and see their past in a different way, it gives the client more freedom to behave differently in general and in sexually, in particular.

As one example, I conducted a sexual history with a client named Dawn, who had experienced sexual trauma as a child. She was molested by a janitor in her school when she was ten years old. Her parents leapt into action once they found out and took control by reporting it to the authorities. For a long time, Dawn had a checklist of all the things they did right: "Well, I'm lucky. I told my parents and they didn't doubt me. They took me to the police station and reported it." It all looked good on paper, but the downside was that they never helped Dawn with her feelings about what happened. It was as if they wanted to sweep the incident under the rug. Emotional processing in her family was discouraged. If she or her siblings expressed feelings, they were told they were being overly dramatic.

It was hard for Dawn to get in touch with her anger and come to terms with the lack of parental emotional nurturing. Dawn never got to process her feelings with her parents and, as a result, her feelings went underground. She entered individual therapy to understand why she was sexually shut down with her boyfriend. She attributed it only to the impact of the molestation.

Dawn is an example of how someone can shut down sexually in adulthood as the result of childhood trauma. However, more specifically Dawn realized her shutdown was not simply the result of the molestation, but more importantly because of the absence of emotional processing with her parents. She discovered an underlying narrative that it's better to keep one's feelings private because it will burden others to share them.

This case presents an important lesson because some therapists take a reductionist view that abuse itself is the core issue in adult sexual problems. For some people it's not the trauma itself that shuts them down as much as the lack of opportunity to work through the feelings about what happened. A caregiver's emotional response (or lack thereof) to a trauma can be just as damaging as the trauma itself.

There is good news in Dawn's story. She was able to change and redefine her narratives. Before therapy, she never considered that her parents played a major role in her trauma, that their failure to comfort her was, in a sense, a second violation.

In short, Dawn was working with two narratives, one conscious and the other unconscious. One was a narrative of being victimized and not really having many options to live a more sexually pleasurable life. But through NRST, she discovered a new option – that she was a survivor who could rewrite her negative narrative about emotions. She learned she could be intentional about her sexual and emotional life with others, especially her boyfriend. As she shared more feelings with her boyfriend, sexuality felt safer and more pleasurable.

Dawn couldn't change the fact that a school janitor had assaulted her. What she *could* take responsibility for was exploring how her narratives about that experience curtailed her sexual agency and her involvement with emotional processing. She had the ability to reclaim as much of the emotional processing as she needed now. She challenged her old frames that sexuality was dangerous and that people don't care about her feelings. And, she ultimately changed the narrative that she was permanently damaged.

She began to own her sexual and emotional experiences and share them with her boyfriend. He was delighted to hear more about her feelings and inner life. He told her it made him feel closer to her. Dawn knew she was embarking on a different emotional and erotic path that was long overdue.

In short, Dawn developed sexual agency despite her experience of trauma. Agency in its simplest form is the ability to act in a way that accomplishes one's goal. Sexual agency is taking action in defining yourself sexually, wherever you fall on the spectrum, from heterosexual to homosexual, from highly interested in sex to asexual. It's about developing an active authentic relationship to sexuality.

The Cultural Roots of Erotic Empowerment

Sexual agency and erotic empowerment have deep roots across many socio-political movements, including the sexual revolution of the 1960s and the civil, feminist, and gay/lesbian rights movements of the 1960s and '70s. The sexual barndoor was flung open in 1972 by the publication of two bestselling books, *The Joy of Sex* by Alex Comfort and *Open Marriage* by Nena and George O'Neill (O'Neill & O'Neill, 1972). Edmund White and Charles Silverstein followed suit with *The Joy of Gay Sex* in 1977. And Fritz Klein brought bisexuality out of the closet in 1978 with his seminal book, *The Bisexual Option*.

Women were defining their sexuality apart from men. Authors like Nancy Friday, Erica Jong, and Betty Dodson were exploring and redefining sexuality for women. These authors are just as relevant today, aiding therapists as they help their clients discover and develop intentional pleasure. Female clients still read Nancy Friday's *My Secret Garden*, Erica Jong's *Fear of Flying*, and Betty Dodson's *Sex for One* to become more open to their sexuality. Candida Royalle, founder of Femme Productions, was one of the first women to develop non-coercive porn from a feminist perspective. During the AIDS crisis, Joseph Kramer, founder of the Body Electric School of Erotic Massage, helped gay men be intimate with one another without the risk of sharing bodily fluids.

The civil rights, feminist, and gay/lesbian rights movements gave rise to a powerful community of intersectional voices about how erotic life affects and is affected by race, ethnicity, gender, class, immigration status, sexual/gender identity, and sexual practices.

Lesbian authors of color Audre Lorde, Gloria Anzaldúa (1987), and Cherrie Moraga (1983) wrote eloquently about the challenges of being outsiders and building bridges across identities. Chrystos (1989), a two-spirit lesbian activist, examined themes about feminism and native rights. Marlon Riggs's (1989) groundbreaking film *Tongues Untied* broke silence about gay black men's love for each other and their struggle against racism, homophobia, and marginalization. And self-described queer activists and sex radicals Joan Nestle (1998), Dorothy Allison (1994), and Amber Hollibaugh (2000) broke silence about class, butch/femme, BDSM, sex work, and surviving sexual abuse.

All of these pioneers speak to the interwoven identities, cultures, and experiences that inform the narratives our clients bring to therapy. Therapists should be familiar with their work, and those who have come after them, so they can offer all clients ways to access sexual entitlement, power, and agency. And therapists can also use the wisdom from these pioneers to explore and develop their own sexual agency and self-knowledge, which is crucial to being an effective therapist.

Sex From a Distance: The Power of Fantasy, Porn, and the Sexual Net

When it comes to intentional sexual pleasure, the internet has had a profound effect on our lives. Today, technology allows us to have sex readily and anonymously. No longer do we have to go to bars to find a partner or to a seedy movie theater to watch porn. Women of my generation rarely did that. Today there are thousands of pornographic websites that can be accessed for free. There are chat rooms and porn sites that cater to every kind of erotic desire and fantasy. There are apps that allow us to find partners by swiping our phones. Online sex enables single people, especially those who are not in urban areas, to experience a diverse world of sexual and social possibilities. This can be lifesaving for an LGBTQ adolescent who's growing up isolated without a queer local community.

Today, some of the largest consumers of online porn are women, and this makes sense because it has what we call the "Triple A": accessibility, affordability, and anonymity (Cooper, 1998). You can safely view it in the privacy of your home, and it doesn't cost much. That's ideal for many women when it comes to intentional pleasure. Sex at a distance can be positive for many people for different reasons.

But as with any technology, there's a potential downside. Many people have valid concerns about the negative impact technology has on our relationships and society, and rightly so. Millions of young people are regularly exposed to porn on their phones, and addiction is a real concern. Compulsive porn use can interfere with a balanced life, negatively affecting work or romantic relationships. Porn use is sometimes a factor in couple conflict, sometimes leading to divorce. (For a sex positive approach to out of control sexual behavior, see Braun-Harvey & Vigorito [2015].)

Some therapists might say: "Internet sex is not real sex. It's a delusion. Real sex is body-to-body." But the reality is that for many single people, sex at a distance via the internet *is* their sex life. Technology allows a single person to be an intentional sexual being instead of completely forfeiting sexual pleasure. Some clients have told me that the thrill of swiping or being swiped on their phone apps is a large part of their sex life. That kind of technological interaction contributes to feelings of sexual attractiveness, sexual self-esteem, and/or sexual self-confidence. In my view, if used in a healthy way, there's nothing wrong with it. For some people, their online sex life is deeply rich and intimate.

The distance created by technology allows some people to learn about and express their sexuality in intentional ways that aren't necessarily unhealthy. Technology can provide an entry point for people who want to learn how to be more sexual, either alone or with a virtual partner. Some people are turned off by the physical experience of sex. They have aversions to bodily fluids, tastes, and smells. Technological sex enables them to bypass those aversions as they work toward having a more expansive sex life.

Technology also allows some people to bypass emotional obstacles to enjoying sexuality. For some people, virtual online connections feel less risky. They don't have to deal with the challenge of becoming attached to someone and then rejected. By its very nature, the online experience is much more fluid and safe regarding attachment. These ways of being sexual online may be one more avenue for people to explore sexual desires and needs. As a sex therapist in this growing technological world, I believe we need to expand the frame of how we define intimacy.

The Potential for Intimacy in Anonymous Sex

In his book *Dancing Around the Volcano: Freeing Our Erotic Lives: Decoding the Enigma of Gay Men and Sex*, Guy Kettelhack (1996) recounts the story of Kevin, a gay man who once suffered from self-esteem issues because of his body – five feet eight inches and just under three hundred pounds – but who now thinks of himself as sexy and hot as a result of random sexual encounters that, to many therapists, might seem devoid of intimacy. Kevin routinely had anonymous sex in the baths with a man whose name he didn't know. The sex was exciting for both of them. After one particularly arousing encounter, the man told Kevin: "You're one of the hottest guys I've ever had sex with in my life."

Kettelhack comments:

> Kevin at first dismissed this as the ravings of some lunatic who perversely got off on fat guys. "I secretly was thrilled, but it took a long while before I could really register that someone might actually find me hot. . . . It was like the first moment in my life where I'd enjoyed being a physical being. Something released in me. . . . I'll stand in front of the mirror and . . . get off on my own body. And I'm still as fat as ever. But, for the first time, I accept that I'm *here*. . . . Am I some kind of weird narcissist? Maybe. But I feel a lot better now than I did when I couldn't stand the sight of myself."
>
> (p. 34)

Kettelhack goes on to say that anonymous sex can be a powerful way to find the self-acceptance that Kevin experienced:

> This acceptance can widen to a healthier self-love; in fact, achieving the kind of narcissism that Kevin describes is real progress. . . . Sexual exploration can be an important means of finding this necessary self-love; learning that our bodies are more than Armani suits, that they are the full, mysterious, interesting physical manifestation of who we are – this is a heady discovery.
>
> (pp. 35–36)

And Kettelhack would certainly contend that this could apply to everyone, not just gay men.

Many therapists might have a judgmental reaction to public anonymous sex, even if it's practiced using safer sex techniques, viewing it as the opposite of intimate. Kevin had no idea what his partner's name was. Yet the experience felt deeply intimate to him, which led to a kind of spiritual awakening about his body and his sexuality. What could easily be judged as an anonymous, even degrading experience turned out to be healthy and even liberating, another reminder to us about how non-conforming and unpredictable sexuality can be.

Helping Clients Come to Their Sexual Senses

A client might say: "I don't have a partner right now. I'm not yet fully engaged in intentional pleasure, so where do I start?"

They can start where they are. They can become curious about what gives them sexual pleasure. They can explore their five senses and make the transition to physical stimulation. They can claim their sexual birthright.

Each of us has five senses – what we can see, hear, taste, smell, and touch. A client can start thinking about how they experience pleasure through the five senses. Ask your clients to write down the five senses and free associate, through writing, about how they might experience pleasure through them. They can observe how they experience that pleasure over the course of a day or a week and continue to record their responses.

Someone might say, "When I saw the sunset the other night, that felt really pleasurable" or "When I go to a museum and see a Picasso, I'm blown away." It's like going back to childhood when we experienced our senses intensely in the present moment. Masters and Johnson knew the importance of our senses through the development of their sensate focus approach. Masters and Johnson believed that part of the reason why people had sexual problems was because they were thinking too much. It's our bodies, not our heads, that know how to receive pleasure, but we are rarely in our bodies.

For some people, mindfulness is already part of their lives through meditation or yoga practice. Other people are not familiar with mindfulness techniques. Their minds get the better of them, not just in the sexual arena but in every other way as well. Their pleasure is diminished in all aspects of their lives because the mental observer is critiquing, commenting, and judging them. This "noise," as I call it, curtails people's ability to enjoy simple pleasures.

By using mindfulness techniques and connecting more with the body, we can help clients access their sensual selves.

Integrating Solo Sex Into Partnerships

A person's solo sexual life should not necessarily change when they enter a relationship.

Some people are more committed to their sexual development than others. They read a lot about sex, view porn or erotica, or they may enjoy art and literature with sexual themes. Perhaps they educate themselves about sexuality through research or by going to sex clubs. I always ask clients together and separately how they describe their commitment to sexuality and sexual development. How much are they individually committed to that development and how much room does the relationship provide for it?

Some people don't want their partners to feel attraction for other people. They don't want their partners fantasizing or masturbating about someone else. Some people will repress those kinds of feelings. But studies show that couples who remain sexual over the lifespan are usually sexually committed not only to each other but also to their individual development. Sexuality is an important part of their identity and crucial to their health and well-being. Their solo sexual development goes beyond masturbation. They live a life that is committed to sexuality.

When I work with a couple, I'll ask one of the partners, "How often do you masturbate?" That question sometimes gets the following reaction: "Why would I masturbate if I have a partner?" But if that person was fantasizing and masturbating when she was single, why should that change now that she has a partner?

When one partner feels threatened by the other partner masturbating, it raises the issue of differentiation in the relationship. Do they allow for enough separation so that one or both partners can masturbate in addition to enjoying partnered sex? We return to the capacity for compersion, where one can be happy if one's partner is enjoying themselves. It's a perspective that often augments healthy sexuality for a couple.

As mentioned earlier, I instruct clients to initially construct their sexual menu alone without sharing it with their partner. This way they can identify their sexual interests without worrying about their partner's reaction. It opens space for self-exploration and discovery. Only later do they share their sexual menu. This sends a clear message that you have to first discover who you are sexually before you can share your sexuality with another. Only then can you co-create a sexual menu that works for both partners. The menu exercise embodies my perspective that a couple is made up of two individuals, who shouldn't lose their individuality when in a relationship.

Maintaining Sexual Resilience Throughout Life

What does it mean for someone to be sexually resilient over the course of a lifetime?

It means expanding our sexual narratives beyond the standard one of desire, arousal, and orgasm; to embrace intention and willingness not for the purpose of demonizing desire but to explore how to change our relationship to desire. As Buddhist psychotherapist Mark Epstein (2005) suggests, one should view "desire as a teacher" to:

> learn how to use desire instead of being used by it . . . [to be] open to desire so that it becomes more than just a craving for whatever the culture has conditioned us to want.

(p. 8)

Resilience means being flexible. Moving from a performance-based to a connection-based erotic life. It means knowing that no matter what happens physically or emotionally in the bedroom, one can still feel good about the connection, about sex, and about ourselves. It means that if someone suddenly feels anxiety, anger, or sadness during sex, they can still value the parts of the experience that were pleasurable, or even feel good about their willingness to try – bringing curiosity instead of judgment to the experience.

Resilience means recovering from having disappointing sex – sex that falls short of what they want – to figure it out together. The use of humor and playfulness along the way helps clients bring patience and compassion to the experience of learning about and accepting themselves and their partners.

These skills help clients live happier sexual lives. They are able to stay in the present moment – "being in sex" instead of "doing sex" – and not get lost in past bitterness or in anticipating future disappointment. They are able to face sexual challenges in new and constructive ways.

Ultimately, clients have to discover their own understanding of what sexual satisfaction means to them. It's a process of trial and error, of developing a kind of communication that can feel both paradoxical and perfect at the same time.

When old, negative narratives try to sneak back in, clients can learn how to anticipate them. They can learn how to navigate setbacks, disappointments, and other common obstacles.

I often tell clients:

"You're on the right path when you can have 'good bad sex'."

In other words, when they have the skills to fully experience and appreciate sex, however it shows up at any given time. They can start and end sex as a connected erotic team, no matter what transpires. Over time, the connected erotic couple is able to identify when a narrative isn't working, explore why that's so, and, by using the skills they learned in NRST, create new more helpful narratives to continue co-creating the erotic lives they want and deserve.

172

REFERENCES

Albee, E. (2005). *Who's afraid of Virginia Woolf?* New York: New American Library.

Allison, D. (1994). *Skin: Talking about sex, class & literature*. Ithaca: Firebrand Books.

Anzaldua, G. (1987). *Borderlands / La frontera: The new mestizo*. San Francisco: Aunt Lute Books.

Bader, M. (2002). *Arousal: The secret logic of sexual fantasies*. New York: St. Martin's Press.

Basson, R. (2001). Human sexual response cycles. *Journal of Sex and Marital Therapy*, *27*(1), 33–43.

Bion, W. P. (1962). *Learning from experience*. London: Tavistock.

Blumstein, P., & Schwartz, P. (1983). *American couples: Money, work, sex*. New York: William Morrow.

Bollas, C. (1989). *Forces of destiny: Psychoanalysis and human idiom*. Northvale, NJ: Jason Aronson.

Bornstein, K., & Carrellas, B. (2019). Forward. In G. Jacobson, J. Niemira, & K. Violeta (Eds.), *Sex, sexuality, and trans identities*. Philadelphia: Jessica Kingsley Publishers.

Bowlby, J. (1988). *A secure base: Parent-child attachment and healthy human development*. New York: Basic Books.

Braun-Harvey, D., & Vigorito, M. (2015). *Treating out of control sexual behavior: Rethinking sex addiction*. New York: Springer.

Brockman, C. (1998). A feminist view of sadomasochism in the nineties. *In the Family*, *3*(4), 10–15.

Brotto, L. (2018). *Better sex through mindfulness*. Vancouver and Berkeley: Greystone Books.

Brotto, L., & Yule, M. (2017). Asexuality: Sexual orientation, paraphilia, sexual dysfunction, or none of the above? *Archives of Sexual Behavior*, *46*(3), 619–627.

Chivers, M. L. (2005). A brief review and discussion of sex differences in the specificity of sexual arousal. *Journal of Sexual and Relationship Therapy*, *20*(4), 377–390.

Chodorow, N. J. (1994). *Femininities, masculinities, sexualities: Freud and beyond*. Lexington: University of Kentucky Press.

Chrystos. (1989). *Not vanishing*. Vancouver: Press Gang Publishers.

Comfort, A. (1972). *The joy of sex*. New York: Crown Publishing Group.

Cooper, A. (1998). Sexuality and the internet: Into the new millennium. *Cyber Psychology & Behavior*, *1*(2), 187–193. http://doi.org/10.1089/cbp.1998.1.187

Corbett, K. (2009). *Boyhoods: Rethinking masculinities*. New Haven: Yale University Press.

Davies, J. (2006). The times we sizzle, and the times we sigh: The multiple erotics of arousal, anticipation, and release. *Psychoanalytic Dialogues*, *16*(6), 665–686.

DiCeglie, G. R. (1995). From the internal parental couple to the marital relationship. In S. Ruszczynski & J. Fisher (Eds.), *Intrusiveness and intimacy in the couple* (pp. 49–58). London: Karnac.

Dimen, M. (2014). *Sexuality, intimacy and power*. New York: Routledge.

Dodson, B. (1987). *Sex for one*. New York: Crown Publishing Group.

Downs, A. (2012). *The velvet rage: Overcoming the pain of growing up gay in a straight man's world*. New York: Da Capo Lifelong Books.

Ellison, C. R. (2001). Intimacy-based sex therapy: Sexual choreography. In P. J. Kleinplatz (Ed.), *New directions in sex therapy* (p.163). Philadelphia: Brunner-Routledge.

Epstein, M. (2005). *Open to desire: The truth about what Buddha taught*. New York: Gotham Books.

Erichson-Schroth, L. (2014). *Trans bodies, trans selves: A resource for the transgender community*. New York: Oxford University Press.

Fonagy, P. (2008). A genuinely developmental theory of sexual enjoyment and its implications for psychoanalytic technique. *Journal of the American Psychoanalytic Association*, *56*, 11–36.

Freud, S. (1905). Three essays on the theory of sexuality. In J. Strachey (Ed.), *The standard edition of the complete psychological works of Sigmund Freud* (Vol. 7, 1953). London: Hogarth Press.

Friday, N. (1973). *My secret garden: Women's sexual fantasies*. New York: Trident.

Frommer, M. S. (2006). On the subjectivity of lustful states of mind. *Psychoanalytic Dialogues*, *16*, 639–664.

Gagnon, J. H., & Simon, W. (1973). *Sexual conduct: The social sources of human sexuality*. Chicago: Aldine.

Gottman, J. (2015). *Principles for making marriage work*. New York: Harmony Books.

Hahn, T. N. (1992). *Peace in every step: The path of mindfulness in everyday life*. New York: Bantam.

Hall, K. S. K., & Graham, C. A. (Eds.). (2013). *The cultural context of sexual pleasure and problems: Psychotherapy with diverse clients*. New York: Routledge.

Harris, A. (2005). *Gender as soft assembly*. Hillsdale, NJ: The Analytic Press.

Hollibaugh, A. L. (2000). *Dangerous desires: A queer girl dreamimg her way home*. Durham: Duke University Press.

Holter, L. (2017, April 24). The murder rate of transgender women in the U.S. isn't declining. *Refinery29*. Retrieved from www.refinery29.com/en-us/2017/04/151401/transgender-women-murder-rate-us-2017

Iasenza, S. (2004). Passion, play and erotic potential space in lesbian relationships. In A. D'Ercole & J. Drescher (Eds.), *Uncoupling convention: Psychoanalytic approaches to same-sex couples and families* (pp. 139–156). Hillsdale, NJ: The Analytic Press.

Iasenza, S. (2006). Low sexual desire in gay, lesbian, and heterosexual peer marriages. In J. S. Scharff & D. E. Scharff (Eds.), *New paradigms for treating relationships* (pp. 375–383). New York: Jason Aronson.

Iasenza, S. (2010). What is queer about sex? Expanding sexual frames in theory and practice. *Family Process*, *49*(3), 291–308.

Iasenza, S. (2016, January–February). Transforming sexual narratives: From dysfunction to discovery. *Psychotherapy Networker*, *42*(1), 24–31.

Imber-Black, E. (1998). *The secret life of families*. New York: Bantam.

Isay, R. (1994). *Being homosexual: Gay men and their development*. New York: Jason Aronson.

Johnson, S. M. (2004). *The practice of emotionally focused couple therapy: Creating connection* (2nd ed.). New York: Routledge.

Johnson, S. M. (2008). *Hold me tight*. New York: Little, Brown & Co.

Johnson, S. M., Simakhodskaya, Z., & Moran, M. (2018, April). Addressing issues of sexuality in couples therapy: Emotionally focused therapy meets sex therapy. *Current Sexual Health Reports*. https://doi.org/10.1007/s11930-018-0146-5

Jong, E. (1973). *Fear of flying*. New York: Signet.

Kabat-Zinn, J. (1994). *Wherever you go, there you are: Mindfulness meditation in everyday life*. New York: Hyperion.

Kaplan, H. S. (1979). *Disorders of sexual desire*. New York: Brunner, Mazel.

Kaplan, M. (2018). Getting beyond the sexual abuse binary: Discerning sexual agency from sexual coercion. Sex positivity in the time of #MeToo. *Contemporary Psychoanalysis*, 1–11.

Keenan, J. (2016). *Sex with Shakespeare*. New York: William Morrow.

Kernberg, O. (1995). *Love relations: Normality and pathology*. New Haven: Yale University Press.

Kerr, M. E., & Bowen, M. (1988). *Family evaluation*. New York: W. W. Norton.

Kettelhack, G. (1996). *Dancing around the volcano*. New York: Three Rivers Press.

Kinsey, A. C., Pomeroy, W. B., & Martin, C. E. (1948). *Sexual behavior in the human male*. Philadelphia: W.B. Saunders.

Kinsey, A. C., Pomeroy, W. B., Martin, C. E., & Gebhard, P. H. (1953). *Sexual behavior in the human female*. Philadelphia: W.B. Saunders.

Klein, F. (1978). *The bisexual option*. New York: Harrington Park Press.

Klein, F., Sepekoff, B., & Wolf, T. J. (1985). Sexual orientation: A multi-variable dynamic process. In F. Klein & T. J. Wolf (Eds.), *Two lives to live: Bisexuality in men and women* (pp. 35–49). New York: Harrington Park Press.

Klein, M., & Robbins, R. (1999). *Let me count the ways*. New York: Tarcher.

Kleinplatz, P. J. (2009). The components of optimal sexuality: A portrait of "great sex". *The Canadian Journal of Human Sexuality*, *18*(1–2), 1–13.

Kohut, H. (1966). Forms and transformations of narcissism. *Journal of the American Psychoanalytic Association*, *14*, 243–272.

Kohut, H. (1977). *The restoration of the self*. New York: International Universities Press.

Kreps, D. (2016, December 11). Watch Madonna talk sexism and misogyny in powerful women in music speech. *Rolling Stone*. Retrieved from www.rollingstone.com/music/music-news/watch-madonna-talk-sexism-misogyny-in-powerful-women-in-music-speech.html

Laws, J. L., & Schwartz, P. (1977). *Sexual scripts: The social construction of female sexuality*. Hinsdale, IL: Dryden Press.

Lev, A. I. (2004). *Transgender emergence*. New York: Haworth Press.

Lorde, A. (1984). *Sister outsider*. Trumanberg, NY: The Crossing Press.

Loulan, J. (1984). *Lesbian sex*. San Francisco: Spinsters, Aunt Lute.

Maltz, W. (1991). *Sexual healing journey: A guide for survivors of sexual abuse*. New York: Harper Perennial.

Masters, W. H., & Johnson, V. E. (1966). *Human sexual response*. Boston: Little Brown.

McCarthy, B. W., & Metz, M. E. (2008). The "good enough sex" model: A case illustration. *Journal of Sexual and Relationship Therapy*, *23*(3), 227–234.

McCarthy, B. W., & Wald, L. M. (2013). Mindfulness and good enough sex. *Journal of Sexual and Relationship Therapy*, *28*(1), 39–47.

McDougall, J. (1995). *The many faces of eros: A psychoanalytic exploration of human sexuality*. New York: W. W. Norton.

Mitchell, S. A. (2002). *Can love last? The fate of romance over time*. New York: W. W. Norton.

Mona, L. R., Cameron, R. P., & Cordes, C.C. (2017). Disability culturally competent sexual healthcare. *American Psychologist*, *72*(9), 1000–1010.

Moraga, C. (1983). *Loving in the war years*. Boston: South End Press.

Morin, J. (1995). *The erotic mind*. New York: Harper Perennial.

Moser, C. (2016). Defining sexual orientation. *Archives of Sexual Behavior*, *45*(3), 505–508.

Moser, C., & Kleinplatz, P. J. (Eds.). (2006). *Sadomasochism: Powerful pleasures*. New York: Harrington Park Press.

Nagoski, E. (2015). *Come as you are*. New York: Simon & Schuster.

Nelson, T. (2013). *The new monogamy*. New York: New Harbinger Press.

Nestle, J. (1998). *A fragile union*. San Francisco: Cleis Press.

Nichols, M. (2006). Psychotherapeutic issues with "kinky" clients: Clinical problems, yours and theirs. *Journal of Homosexuality, 50*(2/3), 281–300.

O'Neill, G., & O'Neill, N. (1972). *Open marriage*. New York: M. Evans & Company.

Oppenheimer, M. (2011, June 30). Married with infidelity. *New York Times*.

Ortmann, D. M., & Sprott, R. A. (2013). *Sexual outsiders: Understanding BDSM sexualities and communities*. New York: Rowman & Littlefield Publishers.

Perel, E. (2006). *Mating in captivity*. New York: Harper Collins.

Person, E. S. (1988). *Dreams of love and fateful encounters: The power of romantic passion*. New York: Penguin Books.

Riggs, M. (1989). *Tongues untied*. Aired on PBS POV Series, July 15, 1991.

Ryan, C., & Jetha, C. (2011). *Sex at dawn*. New York: Harper Perennial.

Samuels, H. (2007, May 7). Sex stereotypes of African-Americans have a long history. *NPR Interview*. Retrieved from www.npr.org/templates/story/story.php?storyId=10057104

Scheinkman, M. (2005). Beyond the trauma of betrayal: Reconsidering affairs in couple therapy. *Family Process, 44*(2), 227–244.

Schiedel, B. (2018, October 10). Babies do masturbate. *Today's Parent*. Retrieved from www.todaysparent.com/baby/baby-health/do-babies-masturbate/

Schnarch, D. (1991). *Constructing the sexual crucible: An integration of sexual and marital therapy*. New York: W. W. Norton.

Schwartz, P. (1994). *Love between equals: How peer marriage really works*. New York: Free Press.

Sheff, E. (2015). *The polyamorists next door*. New York: Rowman & Littlefield Publishers.

Silverstein, C., & White, E. (1977). *The joy of gay sex*. New York: Crown Publishing Group.

Simon, W., & Gagnon, J. H. (1986). Sexual scripts: Permanence and change. *Archives of Sexual Behavior, 15*(2), 97–120.

Sohn, A. (2015, July 1). First comes sex talk with these renegades of couples therapy. *New York Times*.

Stoller, R. J. (1979). *Sexual excitement: Dynamics of erotic life*. New York: Pantheon.

Stoller, R. J. (1985). *Observing the erotic imagination*. New Haven: Yale University Press.

Taormina, T. (2008). *Opening up*. San Francisco: Cleis Press.

Tiefer, L. (1995). *Sex is not a natural act*. Boulder: Westview Press.

Weiner, L., & Avery-Clark, C. (2017). *Sensate focus in sex therapy*. New York: Routledge.

White, M. (1989). *Selected papers*. Adelaide: Dulwich Centre Publications.

White, M. (1995). *Re-authoring lives: Interviews and essays*. Adelaide: Dulwich Centre Publications.

White, M. (2007). *Maps of narrative practice*. New York: W. W. Norton.

Willi, J. (1977). *Couples in collusion*. New York: Jason Aronson.

Wincze, J. P., & Carey, M. P. (1991). *Sexual dysfunction: A guide for assessment and treatment*. New York: Guilford.

Winnicott, D. W. (1971). *Playing and reality*. New York: Tavistock.

INDEX

For Product Safety Concerns and Information please contact our EU
representative GPSR@taylorandfrancis.com
Taylor & Francis Verlag GmbH, Kaufingerstraße 24, 80331 München, Germany

www.ingramcontent.com/pod-product-compliance
Lightning Source LLC
Chambersburg PA
CBHW050653280326
41932CB00015B/2893